PRACTISING INSIGHT MEDIATION

A practical companion to the much-acclaimed *Transforming Conflict through Insight*, *Practising Insight Mediation* examines how insight mediators do their work and why they do it that way. In the book, Cheryl A. Picard, co-founder of insight mediation, explains how the theory of cognition presented in Bernard Lonergan's *Insight* can be used as the basis for a learning-centred approach to conflict resolution in which the parties involved improve their self-understandings and discover new and less threatening patterns of interaction with each other.

Practising Insight Mediation features a wide range of valuable resources for any conflict practitioner, including in-depth descriptions of insight communication skills and strategies, a transcribed example of mediation, sample documents, and a mediator's self-assessment tool. The essential handbook for those interested in learning about and applying this fast-growing conflict resolution and mediation approach, the book also includes discussions of the latest research into the application of the insight approach to areas including policing, spirituality, and genocide prevention.

CHERYL A. PICARD is professor emeritus in the Department of Law and Legal Studies at Carleton University. She now lives in Prince Edward Island, where she spends time lecturing nationally and internationally on the insight approach to conflict and insight mediation.

Practising Insight Mediation

CHERYL A. PICARD

UNIVERSITY OF TORONTO PRESS
Toronto Buffalo London

ISBN 978-1-4426-2937-0

∞ Printed on acid-free, 100% post-consumer recycled paper with
vegetable-based inks.

Library and Archives Canada Cataloguing in Publication

Picard, Cheryl Ann, author
Practising insight mediation/Cheryl A. Picard.

Includes bibliographical references and index.
ISBN 978-1-4426-2937-0 (cloth)

1. Conflict management.   2. Mediation.   3. Insight.   4. Lonergan, Bernard J.F.
(Bernard Joseph Francis), 1904–1984. Insight.   I. Title.

HM1126.P52 2016   303.6'9   C2015-907808-3

University of Toronto Press acknowledges the financial assistance to its
publishing program of the Canada Council for the Arts and the Ontario Arts
Council, an agency of the Government of Ontario.

Canada Council   Conseil des Arts
for the Arts   du Canada

ONTARIO ARTS COUNCIL
CONSEIL DES ARTS DE L'ONTARIO
an Ontario government agency
un organisme du gouvernement de l'Ontario

Funded by the   Financé par le
Government   gouvernement
of Canada   du Canada

Canadä

Contents

Acknowledgments

There are many people to whom I am indebted for the realization of this book. Without their patience, willingness to read early drafts, and engage in lengthy conversations about how best to talk about the ideas and skills presented in this book, it might never have come to fruition and be as clear as I believe it is now. They are, of course, too numerous to mention, and trying to do so would run the risk of leaving out some contributors. There are, however, some individuals whose contributions do need special acknowledgment.

First, I want to acknowledge Drs Kenneth Melchin, Jamie Price, and Andrea Bartoli, who co-authored the final chapter of this book. In this chapter, they each offer a new line of analysis and practice that carries forward and transposes some of the central features discussed in the book. I am also indebted to Dr Therese Jennissen, professor of social work at Carleton University, who generously gave of her time to read and edit early drafts of the book. I am also particularly grateful to Marnie Jull, whose comments on the final draft of the manuscript helped clarify and tighten the ideas presented. Janet Barclay, a long-time insight mediation coach and coordinator of the role-play practice group at Carleton University, transcribed the case study video used in the mediation research project, and it was through her efforts that I was able to provide examples for many of the skills I write about.

A number of other individuals, including Robyn Holland Ayoub, Colleen Currie, Linda Gunning, Dianna Mainville, Megan Price, and Helen Taylor, read draft chapters and gave me comments on the content and construction of the written text. For this, I am very grateful. I am also very appreciative of the work Debi Parush did to provide illustrations to support some of the written text. I also thank freelancer

Barry Norris for his copy editing and Daniel Quinlan at the University of Toronto Press.

I am also indebted to the Insight Mediation Coaches group and students in the Graduate Diploma in Conflict Resolution program at Carleton University, as they often served as subjects in my "living lab" for testing and retesting how to use these skills and how to talk about them.

Last, but far from least, I owe many thanks to my husband, Chick Silliphant, who without fail continues to encourage and support my work.

PRACTISING INSIGHT MEDIATION

Chapter One

The Practice of Insight Mediation: Introduction

Practising Insight Mediation is a book about how insight mediators do their work and why they do it that way. Macro broad-scale theoretical ideas about social action and conflict are linked to the micro small-scale communication skills and conflict-resolution strategies that insight mediators use to help parties in conflict. The application of new ideas based on what we now know about insight mediation is the topic of the final chapter of this book.

Insight mediation came to the fore in 2001, and is evolving as theory and practice continue to inform each other and broaden our understanding of human behaviour and conflict intervention. It is likely that future discussions of insight mediation will be articulated somewhat differently from what you will read in this book; if so, they will reflect a deepening understanding of the practice of insight mediation and a welcome progression and unfolding of new ideas.

Practising Insight Mediation is a companion to *Transforming Conflict through Insight*, co-authored with Kenneth Melchin and published in 2008 by the University of Toronto Press. *Transforming Conflict through Insight* describes in depth the theoretical tenets of the insight approach to mediation. In particular it emphasizes Bernard Lonergan's ideas about learning and insight (Lonergan [1957] 1992) – ideas that are foundational to the insight approach to conflict and the practice of insight mediation.

Practising Insight Mediation is a timely publication. Its explanation of skills emerging from insight theory responds to increasing interest in the insight approach and to numerous requests from academics, conflict practitioners, mediators, and students for a comprehensive and accessible text to help them apply the guiding principles behind the insight method. *Practising Insight Mediation* aims to advance both the knowledge and skills of professional mediators, mediation teachers, researchers, and students of mediation. It is comprehensive enough to use as a text in university and college courses, yet accessible enough for use as a training manual in professional development workshops and continuing education classes. The book focuses particularly on practice skills, while providing a theoretical base for understanding conflict and conflict resolution. Its style and applied nature make it understandable to lay audiences and educational for parties involved in mediation. Moreover, the conflict strategies and communication skills elaborated here are life skills that individuals interested in self-improvement can use.

Given the book's skills-based focus, key theoretical ideas are synthesized into short descriptions that illustrate the actions of an insight practitioner. These ideas are repeated in different ways and at various times to reinforce the content being explained. Examples of skills-in-use, often through simulated dialogue, should also increase understanding and lessen misunderstanding. Explanations of the skills highlighted in the book are supported by dialogue from a transcribed one-hour taped simulated mediation session called "The Straw that Broke the Camel's Back."[1] The mediation revolves around a workplace conflict between a manager and a representative of his team of unhappy employees. It portrays a typical, real-life mediation since neither the actions of the mediator nor those of the parties were scripted. Instead, the interactions between the mediator and parties emerged as the latter got into their roles and then drew upon their own personalities, emotions, and values to act out the conflict scenario.

Knowing that skills development is the primary aim of this book, I often write in the first person, especially when the point I want to make could benefit from an explanation that is more personal and experiential than academic or theoretical. In these instances, I take the stance of a mediation trainer talking to workshop participants, or a teacher talking to her students, and I draw on many years of experience as a practising mediator. Because of the dual nature of my work as a practitioner

---

1 I would like to extend special thanks to insight mediator and coach Janet Barclay for transcribing the video so it could be shared in this way.

and an academic, it is with the voice of a "pracademic" that I write. Praxis is what academics call this application of knowledge to skills, or the working together of knowledge and skill (Smith 1999, 2011).

Becoming a competent mediator in any approach involves the integration of knowledge and skill. Knowing what to do, and why to do it, allows the practitioner to be responsive and to act with informed intention. Another way of saying this is that it enables the mediator to practise "outside the box," and not be limited to acting in a prescriptive or formulaic manner. Instead, it allows the mediator to be creative, imaginative, and flexible, as well as knowledgeable. These ideals are so important in insight mediation practice that they have been explicated as two behavioural outcomes: acting with emergent creativity,[2] and being responsive with informed intention to both the situation and the individuals involved. Acting intentionally and in an informed way in response to something that has happened is referred to as "responsive intentionality" (Melchin and Picard 2008, 92). Responsive intentionality means that the mediator knowingly and intentionally responds to a party based on what he or she sees and has learned about human interaction, rather than on the basis of prescribed steps. I talk more about this in Chapter Two.

Much of what I describe in this book about insight mediation reflects good mediation practice, regardless of the model used. Different models, however, rely upon different practices based on differing world views, which I talk about in Chapter Three. For now suffice it to say that insight mediators, transformative mediators (Bush and Folger 2004), and narrative mediators (Winslade and Monk 2000) all draw upon a relational view of the world. Interest-based mediators (Fisher and Ury 1981), on the other hand, hold an individualist view of social action. Regardless of one's world view, mediators tend to share the common goal of reducing conflict in the hope of achieving an outcome that is better for all. Inherent in this goal is the belief that differing viewpoints, values, and cultures can coexist in peace.

I share this vision of making the world a better and more peaceful place to live, which is one of my reasons for writing this book. A further

---

2 The concept of emergent creativity has been discussed by scholars such as Goldstein (1999); Kauffman (2008); and Lonergan ([1957] 1992).

motivation is rooted in the belief that people who offer to help others deal with conflict should do them no harm – good intentions are simply not good enough. Another way of thinking about this is that parties should not be worse off for having attended mediation. The material contained in *Practising Insight Mediation* supports the belief that mediators' interventions need to be based on solid practice skills that, in turn, are based on theory and have been tested and refined over time. Mediators need to be well trained and good at their craft. They need to be lifelong learners, and to strive continually to improve their practice. Mediation specialists need to share their knowledge and expertise through conference presentations, teaching, and writing. It is in the spirit of sharing and advancing this field that I have written this book.

The Emergence of Insight Mediation

The practice of insight mediation emerged from a joint research project between Dr Kenneth Melchin, from Saint Paul University, and me that began in early 2001. The first article discussing our work was published in 2003 in *Conflict Resolution Quarterly* (Picard 2003a). Subsequent articles expanded upon the theory and practice of insight mediation.[3] Our research focused on the question, What am I doing when I mediate? Although at first glance this question might have seemed relatively simple, it was quite complex, personal, and important.

The question was important because, although mediators say they shape their interventions based on the nature of the dispute and needs of the parties, they can do this only within the realm of their own implicit theories about conflict and human behaviour and their own cultural system of values and beliefs (Sargent, Picard, and Jull 2011). Communication techniques and strategies are part and parcel of our cultural makeup. How we talk and what we hear are dictated by the cognitive maps that drive our actions.[4]

---

3 See Melchin and Picard (2008); Picard and Melchin (2007); Picard and Siltanen (2013); Sargent, Picard, and Jull (2011).

4 Cognitive maps are produced from experience and, over time, take the form of rules and heuristics. In turn these rules act on us as internal and unthinking conventions for our actions. See Berger and Luckmann (1966); Goffman (1974); Tolman (1948).

Some of the complexity of the question was due to the fact that I have worked as a mediator since 1978, and many of the principles supporting my actions had become so internalized that they were no longer in my conscious mind, and thus not easy to make explicit. Like many other mediation practitioners of that era, I was self-taught. In my case I was heavily influenced by my professional background as an educator and social worker and by my personal background as a Canadian, white, middle-class, young woman. And unlike today, when there is a plethora of mediation texts and graduate-level studies on the topic of mediation, then there were few published books and few courses on mediation. In fact, during the 1970s, 1980s, and into the 1990s, mediation was considered more of an art than a science (Picard 2002), and thus being "good at it" was every bit as good as being "educated" about it. Working as a conflict specialist was seen as being part of a social movement to change institutions of justice, with the goal of returning communities to places where people cared for each other, thus creating a world that was at peace instead of at war. That vision still exists today, but in mediation's social and legal institutionalization, it has lost some of its original informality, flexibility, and creativity. Many of today's practitioners view mediation as a job – albeit an important one – rather than as a life calling dedicated to changing unjust social and legal institutions (Picard 2003b).

It was after Bush and Folger published *The Promise of Mediation* in 1994, and after fifteen years of practising and teaching mediation, that I really started to question my work as a mediator. Many of the questions Bush and Folger raised resonated with me, and motivated me to read about different mediation styles and approaches. I attended workshops led by the individuals who were writing thought-provoking texts. I wanted to know who I was as a mediator, and I wanted to be sure I was helping people, not hurting them.

Like Bush and Folger and others, I believed that mediation was more than problem solving. It had an interactive, emotional, and relational component that could change people's lives for the better. Although I knew this intuitively, I could not explain why. The theory behind my practice had become too internalized. I did what I did because it worked; I rarely questioned why or how. My growing desire to study mediation was what led me to focus my doctoral dissertation on its sociological meanings (Picard 2000). As a result of this research I was able to engage at a more theoretical level and with other practitioner-theorists on mediation practices; now it was time to understand "me" in my practice. And so my quest began.

It was to my friend and colleague from Saint Paul University in Ottawa, Kenneth Melchin, that I turned. Over lunch I spoke of my interest in learning more about my mediation beliefs and style. His response was an emphatic, "Cheryl, I know what you do when you mediate, you mediate to get insights." Although at the time this seemed obvious and not all that revealing, by the end of our lunch we had made a commitment to engage in a joint research project designed to bring to the surface the underlying theory, values, and principles behind my mediation practice. We agreed that our theoretical guide would be Bernard Lonergan and his theory of cognition published in the 1950s in a manifesto called "Insight."[5] We chose Lonergan because Ken was convinced that mediation was all about "getting insights." As an esteemed scholar of Lonergan's work, he was the perfect research partner.

The first step we undertook was to videotape an hour-long mediation role-play of a co-worker dispute in which I was the mediator. This dispute between "Danny and Teresa" became the focal point of our analysis, and we used it to exemplify points in our early writing and publications. We chose our research collaborators with care. The first decision was to select who would play the roles of the disputing parties. We wanted to use a mediator who was trained by someone other than me, as this might offer a different mediation perspective. We were fortunate to have Teresa Jantz join our team. Teresa had been trained in Toronto and was a volunteer mediator in a community-based mediation service. After moving to Ottawa she worked as a researcher with Statistics Canada, and provided additional research skills for the project. We agreed the other role-player party should have no training in mediation, but should have some knowledge of Lonergan's work. Danny Lyonnaise, a colleague of Ken's studying Lonergan and a working professional in the areas of facilitation and organizational development, was the perfect fit. In addition to these two individuals, Morag McAleese, also a colleague of Ken's studying Lonergan's ideas at Saint

---

5 Bernard Lonergan (1904–84) was a Canadian Jesuit priest and philosopher who, among other things, elaborated ideas on cognition and insight. The theoretical underpinnings of insight mediation are strongly influenced by Lonergan's work on how humans learn and come to know something to be true.

Paul University, joined the team. She expressed a keen interest in working on the project because it was related to her academic studies; we were delighted to have her join us.

This team of five worked many hours each week over the course of a year reviewing the taped mediation, asking questions of ourselves about why the mediator and the parties did what they did, and noticing in minute detail actions that would have otherwise likely have gone unnoticed, unquestioned, and unexplained. Ken, Morag, and Danny made links to Lonergan's ideas that revealed patterns in both the mediator's and the parties' actions, while Teresa and I focused on the mediation strategies that seemed to provoke particular interactions between the parties or with the mediator. Ken and I took all these data, and together we began to articulate a theoretical explanation for actions that hitherto had been more intuitive and reactionary than understood and intentional.

We discovered that some of the strategies and interactions we observed were being discussed in the mediation literature, while others were not. It was the interventions that appeared to be distinct that most caught our attention and became the focus of our ongoing research. As our work progressed it became clear that, if we were to engage with the literature and be in conversation with other conflict theorists and mediation practitioners, we needed to articulate these differences and distinguish our approach from those of others. We had to find a different name for what we were doing. "Insight mediation" seemed the right fit given its link to Lonergan, our theoretical guide, and his work on learning and the power of insight.

Some of the ideas about insight mediation practice discussed in this book came out of this initial research, while other ideas have emerged, and deepened, from ongoing research and reflective practice over the past decade. We have been able to deepen and apply our knowledge through the use of a circular research strategy that began with our initial "practice-to-theory" investigation. Following from this initial work, we engaged in a "theory-to-practice" strategy that linked insight ideas with broader theories of social action and change. We then shared these advancements in practice and knowledge at conferences and used them in our classrooms and private mediation practices, which enabled us to provide an even deeper theoretical articulation of insight mediation and a refinement of its practice. This circular "practice-to-theory" and "theory-to-practice" research strategy not only continues;

it also involves additional researchers in investigating different realms of application.[6]

The exploration and subsequent development of insight mediation began as a personal quest to understand my work as a mediator. It has since developed into substantially more. Other practitioners in other countries now identify themselves as insight mediators.[7] New literature continues to be published, and more academics are focusing attention on this topic, not only in the area of mediation but more broadly on the emergence and nature of conflict itself. This broader focus is referred to as the "insight approach to conflict," and is being applied in various conflict interventions, including negotiation, conflict coaching, facilitation restorative justice, and group conflict.

Inherent in all of this work are a number of still-to-be-answered questions: In what types of conflict are the insight approach to conflict and insight mediation applicable? What are the limits? How can the idea of learning and insight be applied in more diverse conflict contexts? What do other approaches have to offer this developing model?

Given our initial research, we are confident that insight mediation can be an effective method in many interpersonal and small-group conflicts. It has shown itself to be a particularly powerful approach where there are ongoing relations and deeply rooted values – most notably in family, elder, workplace, church, community, and cross-cultural disputes, where healing and reconciliation are key to bringing about lasting change. That said, we believe we have only skimmed the surface in knowing if, and how, the theory and practice of insight mediation might also be useful as an agent of change in more transactional and business-like disputes or in instances of violent and deadly conflict.

---

6 For instance, Dr Andrea Bartoli, Dean of the School of Diplomacy and International Relations, Seton Hall University, has applied insight ideas to genocide prevention; Dr James Price, Director of the Sargent Shriver Peace Institute, has used the skills and concepts in a project on police retaliation; Neil Sargent, a professor in the Department of Law and Legal Studies, Carleton University, has focused his writing on insight negotiation and large-scale group conflicts; and Marnie Jull, a PhD candidate in the Department of Sociology, Carleton University, is investigating the experience of insight through intersubjectivity.

7 In addition to individuals from across Canada and the United States, insight mediation practitioners can be found in Trinidad and Tobago and in Bermuda, as insight mediation training in these countries has been taking place over the past few years.

This is not to suggest that insight mediation is some kind of panacea, just that attention to its use in other areas of conflict has yet to be paid. As the approach draws more attention from practitioners and researchers, answers to these questions will begin to emerge. It is my hope that this book, together with its predecessor, *Transforming Conflict through Insight*, will provide the resources to support this important work.

The Outline of the Book

In Chapter Two I provide an introduction to the method of insight mediation. I begin with how conflict is defined in the literature and how these definitions differ from the insight definition of conflict. Emanating from how conflict is defined in the insight approach, I examine a core statement of insight mediation practice and its theoretical footings.

An important element of insight mediation practice is its distinguishing between "defend stories" and "threat stories," and in Chapter Two I articulate this difference and how it comes into play. Insight mediators are taught to focus less on parties' defend stories, and instead to explore the threats to their care stories. Embedded in threat stories are levels of value that are thought to be at risk. Based on the work of Lonergan ([1957] 1992), three such levels are: 1) goals, interests, desires, and human needs; 2) expected patterns of interpersonal interactions; and 3) judgments about appropriate social relations (Melchin and Picard 2008). In the insight approach, surfacing and working with one or more of these levels of value is the key to changing the conflict situation. I also discuss another key feature of insight mediation: "responsive intentionality," which involves the mediator in a twofold process of following the parties as they tell their stories, and then responding to each party individually in an intentional and informed way.

In Chapter Three I explain Lonergan's method of self-understanding and gaining insight into insight, as these ideas have given rise to many of the communication skills and conflict-resolution strategies insight mediators use. The learning process that allows us to come to know and understand an event engages us in four distinct operations: 1) experience; 2) understanding; 3) judgment; and 4) decision (Melchin and Picard 2008, 56). I explain each of these four operations, as well as what we mean by insight and the generation of insight, since these play a key role in the work of insight mediators. In this chapter I also draw readers' attention to some of the distinct practices of insight mediation, including: 1) noticing and wondering about defensive patterns of interaction;

2) deepening the understanding of threats-to-cares in order to understand defend responses; 3) recognizing that feelings are carriers of values; 4) recognizing the three levels of value and their hierarchical nature; and 5) beginning the mediation process by asking about hopes, rather than issues. In the latter part of the chapter I touch upon the difference between a relational world view and an individualistic view, demonstrating the influence of these differences by contrasting the insight approach with the interest-based approach to mediation (Fisher and Ury 1981). To further situate these views and their links to mediation practice, I touch upon some of the differences between insight mediation and transformative mediation (Bush and Folger 1994, 2004) and narrative mediation (Winslade and Monk 2000).

In Chapter Four I detail the five phases of insight mediation: 1) attending to process; 2) broadening understanding; 3) deepening insights; 4) exploring possibilities; and 5) making decisions. I use dialogue from the simulated mediation, "The Straw that the Broke the Camel's Back," used in the original research that gave rise to this approach, to situate the interactions of the parties with the mediator's actions, thus providing concrete examples of what particular skills-in-use would sound like and produce. I also talk briefly about the practice of caucusing, and in Appendix B provide some suggestions for holding one. A caucus is when the mediator has a private meeting with each of the parties during the mediation session. Caucusing is a strategy commonly used in many mediation models (Hoffman 2011), but in insight mediation it is used only a last resort, given the insight mediator's focus on surfacing interpretation to advance learning, a focus that requires the parties to talk face-to-face so that *mis*understanding, *mis*interpretation, and *mis*information can be noticed more easily. Despite its infrequent use, it is still important for insight mediators to know why and how to caucus in the event that it is the only way for parties to continue their dialogue. In describing making decisions, the last phase of insight mediation, I touch upon outcome decisions and the documents used to record them.

In Chapter Five I discuss what happens "before and the after" insight mediation. I begin with a description of pre-mediation – commonly referred to as the convening phase of mediation. I conclude with a discussion of post-mediation and follow-up, as well as how to ensure that parties make informed decisions about participating in mediation. Appendix C presents a sample "Consent to Participate in Mediation" document.

Chapter Six describes some of the more distinctly micro communication skills that insight mediators use. They include deepening the learning conversation, exploring meaning-making and interpretation; being transparent; bridging listening and exploring, finishing the conversation and using the information; linking thoughts and actions; delinking misunderstanding; and verifying insight. I also discuss communication skills that would be familiar to most any mediator, including immediacy, confronting discrepancy, normalizing, asking for feedback, temperature taking, and using verbal cushions.[8]

In Chapter Seven I discuss recent achievements of and future hopes for the insight approach to conflict from the viewpoint of three highly respected scholars: Dr Andrea Bartoli, Professor and Dean, School of Diplomacy and International Relations, Seton Hall University, and former dean of the School for Conflict Analysis and Resolution, George Mason University; Dr James Price, Director, Sargent Shriver Peace Institute and Research Professor in the School for Conflict Analysis and Resolution, George Mason University; and Dr Kenneth Melchin, Professor and Director, Lonergan Centre, Saint Paul University.

It is my hope that, after reading these seven chapters in what is primarily a skills-based book grounded in easily understood theories about learning and conflict resolution, readers will learn new communication, conflict resolution, and mediation skills, and improve upon their existing skills. Through the use of concrete case examples, explanations of terms, skills, and strategies, and a bibliography, students of mediation and anyone interested in bettering their lives should find this book a useful resource.

---

8 Some of these skills and others are discussed in Folberg and Taylor (1984); and Moore (2003).

Chapter Two

Insight Mediation:
Helping Parties in Conflict Learn about
Themselves in Relation to Others

In this chapter I examine four theoretical footings that support the practice of insight mediation, as well as features that distinguish insight mediation practice from other approaches to conflict resolution. To begin, I present some general definitions of conflict, and then contrast these with how insight practitioners define conflict.

Defining Conflict

How conflict and its resolution are defined has a significant impact on how the mediator interacts with parties in mediation. Although contemporary definitions vary, many tend to share the notion that conflict is about achieving "power over" others. We see this in the use of words such as incompatibility, competition, struggle, and defeat. To cite some examples, Coser (1968, 232) explains conflict as "a struggle over values or claims to status, power and scarce resources, in which the aims of the conflicting parties are not only to gain the desired values but also to neutralize, insure or eliminate their rivals." Boulding (1962, 5) defines conflict as a "situation of competition in which the parties are aware of the incompatibility of the potential future position and in which each party wishes to occupy a position which is incompatible with the wishes of the other." Hocker and Wilmot (1995, 21) view conflict as "an expressed struggle between at least two interdependent parties who perceive incompatible goals, scarce resources, and interference from others in achieving their goals." Deutsch (1973, 10) defines conflict as "existing whenever incompatible activities occur." And Himes (1980, 14) describes conflict as "the purposeful struggles between collective actors who use social power to defeat or remove opponents and to gain status, power resources and scarce values."

Human needs conflict theorists such as John Burton (1990a,b) argue that a primary cause of protracted or intractable conflict is people's unyielding drive to meet their unmet needs on individual, group, and societal levels. Many large-scale conflicts exemplify human needs conflict because they involve the unmet needs of identity and security, making conflict resolution difficult because needs cannot be traded, suppressed, or bargained for. The human needs approach supports collaborative and multifaceted problem-solving models and related techniques to resolve conflict.

Although there is a great deal of overlap between what Burton talks about as needs and what insight mediators have labelled "cares," insight mediators think of conflict somewhat differently. The focus of their attention is on action as a defensive response to apprehensions of threat (see Melchin and Picard 2008; Price 2013), rather than on action as intent to meet needs. Defend responses protect against perceived unwelcome and dire outcomes, and can generate a sense of threat in the other party and an ensuing defend response. The degree to which one party defends is influenced directly by the degree of threat to what is valued (Price 2013, 119). Over time these defend responses become the parties' predominant pattern of interaction, which creates, escalates, and sustains the conflict. When the relations between valuing and defending change, so too will defend patterns of interaction change. In other words, changing the pattern will change the conflict. The goal of an insight mediator, then, is to engage the parties in a learning process that changes defend patterns of interaction.

The Insight Definition of Conflict

In the insight approach, conflict is defined as emerging from the experience that one party's actions pose a threat to another's deeply held values, which triggers a defensive response. This response, because it is "self-focused," not "other-focused," seems to others like an attack, and so they, too, respond defensively. Conflict results from ongoing defend patterns of interaction (see Figure 1).

To change the conflict situation, the parties need to identify and understand their threat experiences, defend responses, and patterns of interaction differently. New understandings are produced through dialogue that makes room for parties to wonder about how to change the situation, rather than merely to defend from it. Put another way, the de-escalation of the threat, brought about through a transformation of understanding, produces a new attitude that enables the parties to find

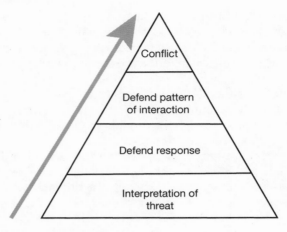

Figure 1: The Emergence of Conflict

ways to resolve their differences or to live more peacefully with them (see Figure 2). Defining conflict in this way gives rise to the following statement of practice that guides insight mediators (see Figure 3):

> *Conflict emerges when individuals or groups experience threats to their desires and needs, expected patterns of cooperation, or deeply held judgments about social order that lead them to respond defensively. Defend responses feel like threats to others, and they, too, respond defensively, thus creating defend patterns of inter-action that sustain the conflict. Through deepening conversations, the mediator assists the parties to gain insight that produces new understandings and alters defend patterns of interaction, so that learning and change can occur.*

The Practice of Insight Mediation

Four conceptual footings support the above statement on insight mediation practice:

1) Conflict emerges from responding defensively to experiences of threat.
2) Threats emerge from interpretations that other's actions will have unwelcome or dire consequences.

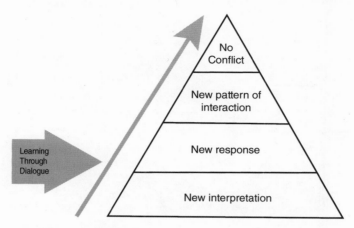

Figure 2: Learning through Dialogue

3) Conflict escalates and is sustained through the ongoing defend patterns of interaction used to protect against experiences of threat.
4) The insight produced through dialogue allows for the discovery of new and less threatening patterns of interaction that can change the conflict situation for the better.

Let's look more closely at each of these ideas, since they form the operating system for insight mediation practice (see Figure 3).

1. Conflict emerges from responding defensively to experiences of threat

As defined in Chapter One, conflict is understood as emerging from an interpretive experience of threat. More specifically, it is a threat to one or more deeply held values. To distinguish the depth and breadth of these values from a more commonplace use of the term "values," early insight advocates adopted the term "cares" when referring to values and "threats-to-cares" when those values were perceived as threatened.

Cares are deeply held beliefs that exist on a personal, relational, and social level that have developed over time from personal experiences and cultural influences. Cares motivate action. In conflict situations, they are what motivate parties to defend, sometimes at any cost. Cares include interests, needs, and desires, as well as the scores of ways in

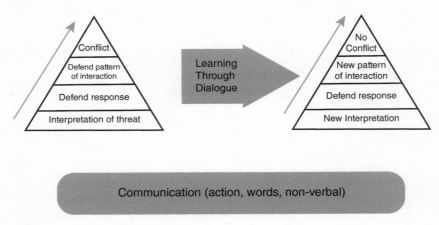

Figure 3: Insight Mediation Practice

which we identify ourselves, our families, our professions, and our culture, including our religious, political, and social beliefs. For parties in conflict, they are at the root of what really matters and what needs to be protected. Threats-to-cares provide explanations for parties' behaviour.

Cares are more than the act of caring. They are values that exist at three hierarchical levels that move from the personal to the relational to the social (Melchin and Picard 2008, 70): 1) personal desires; 2) normative patterns of interaction with others; and 3) judgments about the progress of society. Let's look at each of these three levels more closely.

1. PERSONAL DESIRES

individual

Personal desires include personal goals, needs, and interests. They are the lowest level of values that people hold, and although we can feel strongly about them and they can be strong motivators of human action, they lose priority when values about normative patterns of interaction and relations are challenged. For example, we might not want to head out in inclement weather to vote in a by-election, but we do so because we believe in the importance of the democratic process. Or, against our wishes, we agree to paint our daughter's room purple because we want her to learn to make her own decisions and to let her know that we love and support her. Or we trade our upcoming vacation week with another employee even though we were really looking forward to the break because we know it will be good for workplace relations.

(handwritten margin note: axiorship)

2. NORMATIVE PATTERNS OF INTERACTION WITH OTHERS

Normative, or expected, patterns of interaction with others include the values we place on relationships, such as being a good parent, partner, co-worker, neighbour, teacher, student, friend, and so forth. These second-level cares are about relationships and patterns of cooperation with other individuals, as well as organizations or institutions in which we cooperate with others to achieve goals that benefit all. These relationships carry their own internal obligations that take us beyond our individual desires and needs. Second-level values give us identity.

(handwritten margin note: cultural)

3. JUDGMENTS ABOUT THE PROGRESS OR DECLINE OF SOCIETY

At the highest level of cares are the criteria by which we come to judge what is right and just in the world around us. It is at this level that we subject personal relationships and social institutions to critical scrutiny in relation to human rights, justice, and other unfair social practices.

The discovery and exploration of an individual's threats to his or her cares, commonly referred to as threats-to-cares, requires genuine wondering, skill, and sensitivity on the part of the mediator. Thus, the training of insight mediators involves learning how to facilitate insight into the values-based interpretations that underlie the conflict dynamic. Students of insight mediation are taught to pay particular attention to higher-level cares, as these are the more powerful motivators of human action. When higher-level cares are threatened, resistance to learning and change is strongest. Insight mediators also learn to notice, acknowledge, and explore the expression of strong feelings, for underneath those feelings a care is being threatened. I examine this idea that feelings are carriers of values in the following chapter.

2. Threats emerge from interpretations that others' actions will have unwelcome or dire consequences

Insight mediation is based on an *interpretive* and *interactionist* view of action and communication, which situates human beings as social actors who live their lives within a network of relationships that help form their identity (Sargent, Picard, and Jull 2011, 345). This view of action is taken from Mead (1934), who said we become self-aware by imagining ourselves as others see us. Our values and our perspective of others' perspectives of us influence how we act. In other words, our actions are in relation to others, not independent of others.

Over time our actions, and the actions of others, form "meaning perspectives" that filter the way we understand our day-to-day lives

(Mezirow 1991). Meaning perspectives, or "narratives," are ordered sets of ideas and expectations that have become habitual, to the extent that we rarely are aware of them and how much they shape the way we interpret others and the positions we take in relation to others. These meaning perspectives, then, become the unconscious rules by which we live our lives and how we think others should live their lives. A simple example of this is hearing ourselves give our children the same advice that our parents gave us, even though we remember that we neither wanted nor valued this advice at the time it was given. Our meaning perspective, in this example, has become so habitual over time that we are not even aware of it until we hear our "parents' voices" in the advice we offer our children.

Although meaning perspectives provide the necessary frameworks for living our lives, they can also be problematic, since they are rarely complete. As we go through life, we can develop assumptions and attitudes that distort our understanding of issues, cut off new lines of thinking and questioning, and limit our ability to integrate new ideas. These distortions, which psychologists refer to as "attribution bias,"[1] create resistance to learning and change. Attribution bias is a cognitive bias that refers to the systematic errors people make when they evaluate or try to find reasons for their own and others' behaviour.[2] Parties in conflict almost always make attributions regarding the cause of their own and others' behaviour; however, these attributions do not always accurately mirror others' intentions.

Because actions are responses to the meanings we attribute to interactions and communications with others (Sargent, Picard, and Jull 2011, 347), insight mediators are taught to ask elicitive questions about "interpretation" far more than questions about "intent." Asking elicitive questions is a skill most mediators use. In many models these questions focus on expanding the speaker's known information with minimal confirmation that others understood correctly. In insight mediation there is a concerted attempt right from the start to discover how each other's words and actions are being interpreted. Listeners are asked what they heard the speaker say before the mediator moves on to elicit new information. This is important because so often what listeners hear

---

1 Some of the early work on attribution bias originated from psychologist Fritz Heider in his 1958 book, *The Psychology of Interpersonal Relations*.
2 Social psychologists continue to study this concept; see, for instance, Matthews and Norris (2002); and Zuckerman (1979).

is not what the speaker meant. Surfacing and correcting miscommunication allows new information to be more easily understood correctly. I discuss this strategy in more detail in Chapter Six. For now, here are some examples of interpretive and meaning-making questions.

- What did you just hear her say about the reasons for the actions she took?
- What did you interpret from his refusal to reopen discussions on the topic?
- How did you make sense of the incident?
- What did it tell you when the memo came across your desk that you and your co-workers need to engage in respectful interactions with management?
- How did you interpret his intent when you learned he spoke to your supervisor about the missing files?

Interpretive questions are often followed by asking the speaker to verify if what the listener thinks or heard was what was meant, or if what has been attributed as intent is in fact so. For instance, the mediator might ask:

- How does what he just said fit with your intentions?
- What do you have to say about how she understands what you have been telling us?
- Is what you meant what she understood?
- What, if anything, is missing from what she heard about your reasons for taking the action you did that you really want her to know?
- What more does he need to know to understand your view of things?
- How does her interpretation of your reasons leave you feeling?

Insight mediators explore the interpretation and meaning making of the listener as a strategy to ensure that the intent of the speaker is understood. They do this more often than relying on the speaker to explain his or her intent to the listener. For instance, rather than ask the speaker if what he or she heard was correctly understood, the mediator would ask the listener to tell the speaker what he or she took from what was just said. Theory and experience show that having the speaker explain intent does not necessarily ensure that the listener's interpretation of that intent is actually what the speaker meant. Once again this can be a consequence of attribution bias or cultural or value differences. Misinterpretation can be increased when our constructed narrative convinces us that we know all there is to know, leaving us deaf to new or different information – what is said is often not what is heard, no matter how often it is repeated. This is especially true in conflict situations where the parties' experiences of threat cause a "fight or flight" response,[3] creating ongoing defend patterns of interaction. Defence blocks learning about others because it is so self-focused. Although listening actively to the speaker is a common practice in most models of mediation, listening to the listener is a lesser-used strategy in other models.

Listening to the listener is important for a number of reasons. As long as people are convinced others are out to do harm, it is difficult to open their minds to consider anything that others have to say: they are closed to learning because they are certain they know all there is to know about the other person. This is particularly true in long-standing relationships such as those found in families, communities, or workplaces, where there is plenty of "evidence to prove one right." Over time individuals come to notice only those interactions that reinforce threat-based narratives, placing them even more strongly in the position of "knower" and defender of their "truth." From the position of knower, there is little or no reason to be curious about the other. In fact, being curious can itself pose a threat if one's curiosity is interpreted as a sign of agreement or weakness. Talking might be going on, but the ability to learn about each other is blocked. Insight mediation allows curiosity to emerge by disrupting the certainty of knowing through learning conversations. The uncertainty that is produced, combined with the drive to understand our surroundings, is what expands the base of experience, produces new insight, and changes patterns of interaction. Simply put, through a learning dialogue, insight mediators facilitate the process of learning; this learning is then directed at helping parties discover what is driving their involvement in the conflict and how they might change their responses to it.

Conflict is not only about the present; it also involves interactions that are strongly linked to experiences from the past and to a future that anticipates unwanted and sometimes dire outcomes. Human action is a "response" to something, as much as, if not even more than, the

---

3 "Fight or flight" – also known as the acute stress response – refers to a physiological reaction that occurs in the presence of something that is terrifying, either mentally or physically. The fight or flight response was first described in the 1920s by US physiologist Walter Cannon, who realized that a chain of rapidly occurring reactions inside the body help mobilize the body's resources to deal with threatening circumstances.

"intention" to do something (Sargent, Picard, and Jull 2011, 347). Thus insight mediation explores a party's reactions even more than the party's intentions. And because meaning making is internal, personal, and formed from individual cognitive schemas, insight mediators are not surprised to find that messages have been misunderstood. A basic assumption in insight mediation is that conflicting parties' interpretations of each other's intent are as likely to be wrong as right. Cognitive psychologists explain this phenomenon as happening because meaning making is generated from unique cognitive maps and mental schemas that have formed through past experiences and from situational factors such as culture, background, training, social status, gender, age, ethnicity, and so forth (Berger and Luckmann 1966; Goffman 1974). Our brains use these mental maps as organizing principles that then form our habits, reflexive actions, values, and world views, which then influence how we act. To recognize the power of mental schemas or cognitive maps, we need only recall a time when we were drawn into the middle of our friends' conflict and, after listening to each of them, were left wondering whether they were even in the same conflict because their stories about each other's intentions were so different!

Insight mediators learn that conflicting parties' actions are linked to the way they interpret each other's intent. These interpretations are formed from the words or gestures of others that trigger feelings arising from previous experiences where there was harm. The insight mediator's role thus focuses on discovering whether one's interpretations accurately reflect the other's intent. This can, and often does, lead to the discovery that each other's intent was not only misinterpreted, but that what was intended would have been well received by the other party. Surfacing meaning making often helps parties to make sense of behaviour that previously made little or no sense. Exploring parties' interpretations not only delinks incorrect interpretations; it also offers the possibility of replacing them with more accurate and less threatening knowledge.

3. Conflict escalates and is sustained through the ongoing defend patterns of interaction used to protect against experiences of threat

Understanding that conflict is interpretive leads to the third distinguishing feature of insight mediation: insight mediators pay attention to the parties' patterns of interaction, especially their defend patterns. Defend responses include obvious argumentative expressions such as "that is not what I am saying," or "how can you not get this," or "this is not rocket science; why is it so hard for you to understand!" It also involves listening for the not-so-obvious responses that are framed as "yes, but ...," and subtle responses aimed at "convincing you that I am right" or "getting you to understand."

As previously mentioned, when people feel threatened, their flight or fight response is triggered. Fight or flight responses focus on the self; by their very nature they ignore what might matter to others. To others these defend responses are not simply experienced as rejections but as attacks on them. The response to feeling attacked is to defend. Their fight or flight response in turn feels like an attack back, leaving both parties in defend positions, and so the conflict spirals. I experience your defence as an attack – an attack that you might never have intended or are even unaware that I am experiencing. Thus, to you, my attack makes little or no sense other than as an intended act that forces me to defend against you.

These defend patterns of interaction need to be changed for learning to occur. This is why insight mediators pose questions that they anticipate will assist the parties to expand their knowledge and create insight into why they feel threatened. Insight that lessens experiences of threat serves to empower the parties to discover patterns of interaction that are less threatening. Reducing threats helps the parties refocus their energy. By engaging in a different type of dialogue, they can now turn their minds to discovering new ways of interacting that bring about change for the better.

Insight mediators use a skill called "noticing" to pay attention to whether learning is happening or being blocked. Noticing is a core skill that recognizes the possibility that listeners might take in all the words, yet overlook what is important in the speaker's message. It is a skill that attends to the bigger picture by paying close attention to all that is going on between the parties and between the parties and the mediator, both verbally and non-verbally. Noticing is a skill that involves listening with *both* our ears and our eyes. It requires hypervigilance not unlike walking in the dark of night, when we are unsure of our footing and of what lies ahead. Although at first glance noticing might seem like an obvious mediation skill, to do it well mediators must train themselves to be very present, in the moment, and totally focused on what is going on between the parties and between the parties and themselves. For some people it can be a real challenge not to let their mind wander even for a few seconds.

When the parties are engaged in defend patterns of interaction and communication, we can expect that their learning is being blocked.

Defend interactions become supported by defend stories that reject each other's viewpoints, implying that the other is wrong. Each of the parties is focused on proving and convincing the other that they are right. Defence responses are imbued with explanations, rationales, and details to support the defender's way of viewing things. Ongoing defend conversations leave little hope that new information will be heard, let alone considered. When defending is going on, the parties are generally talking more than listening, unless they have shut down communication altogether.

Mediators trained in the insight approach are taught to differentiate between defend stories and the story that underlies them: the threat story. They intentionally do not explore defend stories because these narratives contain the "rationale for my actions." Exploring this rationale is problematic because it is almost always constructed in ways that blame and judge others, making the information difficult, if not impossible, for others to hear. Insight mediators learn that expanding one party's defend story creates a defend response by the other party, which gets in the way of facilitating productive dialogue. This is not to suggest that the mediator ignores the content of the defend story – in other words, the circumstances, issues, experiences, and emotions of the conflict. This information is necessary to understand why others' actions make sense to them, and the mediator will use it to discover how different actions could improve those circumstances, issues, experiences, and emotions. The point is that insight mediators explore the content of the conflict situation at a time and in a way that conflicting parties are better able to hear each other and then consider what each is saying. More on this below.

4. Insight produced through dialogue allows for the discovery of new and less threatening patterns of interaction that can change the conflict situation for the better

The insight approach understands mediation as an interpretive process of learning. The learning produced through dialogue is the impetus that brings about change. The reverse is also true: through change, learning occurs. Using a learning process instead of a problem-solving process has a profound impact on the actions of the mediator.

Insight mediators, acting on the understanding that conflicts are best solved when conflicting parties are free to learn, see their role as helping to facilitate new insight and understanding by the parties. When the parties gain a new perspective of themselves and each other and of the relations between them, this empowers them to seek new ways of interacting that will address their differences in less threatening ways.

As mentioned in the introduction to this book, the theory of learning used by insight mediators comes from Canadian philosopher, theologian, and economist Dr Bernard Lonergan, whose life work was given to the question: How do we know and, more particularly, how do we come to know what is good?[4] Lonergan, however, was interested in questions of theology, not conflict. Linking his ideas of learning and insight with conflict occurred through the work of Dr Kenneth Melchin, a professor at Saint Paul University in Ottawa. Ken provided the theoretical base for understanding Lonergan's ideas, and together we made this knowledge amendable to application through the practice of insight mediation (Melchin and Picard 2008).

Lonergan tells us that learning takes place in a sequence of four operations that arise from genuine wondering: experience, understanding, judgment, and decision (Melchin and Picard 2008, 56). Learning emerges from questions. Insight is the answer to the question, what is it? and judgment is the answer to the question, is it so? Each of these operations is described in detail in the next chapter, but for now it suffices to explain that, to really know something, we must first obtain the information, then understand what the information means, then ensure that our understanding is correct, and, finally, be able to use the information to act. Learning thus involves much more than the passive reception of information.

Lonergan and other learning theorists such as Jack Mezirow (1990), a leader in the field of transformative learning, contend that the desire to understand the meaning of our experience is a defining condition of being human. It is this desire that produces within us the curiosity needed to engage in dialogue that will generate new insight. In conflict situations this insight leads to discovering new ideas for change.

---

4 Bernard Lonergan (1904–84) was the principal architect of what he called the "generalized empirical method." Born in Buckingham, Quebec, he received a typical Catholic education and eventually entered the Society of Jesus (Jesuits), leading to his ordination to the priesthood in 1936. He specialized in both theology and economics, having been influenced by his doctoral work on Thomas Aquinas and by his long-standing interest in the philosophy of culture and history, honed by his reading of Hegel and Marx. While teaching theology in Toronto, Lonergan wrote his ground-breaking philosophical work, *Insight: A Study of Human Understanding* ([1957] 1992). Then, in 1972, he published his equally fundamental work, *Method in Theology*.

Recall that insight mediation was created by applying Lonergan's principles of learning to the process of conflict mediation. With learning so paramount, the key role of the insight mediator became one of assisting conflicting parties to develop a curiosity about each other and about themselves. Disrupting the certainty of already "knowing" others allows our innate sense of curiosity to generate such questions as "why I am feeling so angry with her?" and "what she is thinking about me?"

Because parties in conflict are so certain that what matters to them is at risk, their attention is focused on protecting their viewpoint, resources, values, identity, person, and so forth. There is little room for curiosity about the other, since each party knows the other only as a threat. It is only through talking and listening differently that the parties are able to hear things in a new way. Curiosity towards self and the other emerges from the uncertainty that is created when something new or different about what they thought they already knew is discovered. The curiosity needed for learning emerges when the certainty of knowing all there is to know is disrupted.

Uncertainty can surface when a mediator asks one party questions about how he or she interpreted the actions of the other party. It is in listening to the answer to these questions that wrong assumptions and misinterpretations are discovered and new understandings produced. Disrupting the certainty of knowing provides an opportunity to explore, correct, and expand misinformation. But conflict is generated not only from misinformation; in a conflict dynamic, there can be the real intention to do harm – an interpreted threat can be very real. In this case disrupting the certainty that *only* a threat exists through parties' interactions is what needs exploring. The insight generated from such a discussion can produce new interpretive frameworks, which enable the parties to seek possibilities for resolution and change.

Insight mediators trigger curiosity between the parties by skilfully facilitating communication between them that reviews what is known, highlights information that is new, ensures that new information is correctly understood, and then helps to synthesize the new connections. In Chapter Six I examine many of the communication skills that insight mediators use to achieve these outcomes.

The Importance of Differentiating between Defend Stories and Threat Stories

An important contribution of the insight method has been distinguishing between exploring different lines of inquiry and which line is more likely to produce new learning and new outcomes. The content of these lines of inquiry has been dubbed "defend stories" and "threat stories."

Defend stories contain parties' rationale for being "right" and for knowing others are "wrong." They are closed stories with no room for change because of the parties' certainty of knowing they are right and justified in acting as they do. Defend stories emerge from trying to make sense of the events and interactions that are integral to the conflict. They are firmly held, sense-making stories that are embedded within a party's sense of self-worth. They are the stories that others involved in the conflict reject and use to justify the need to protect against. They are the stories that fuel the conflict and keep it going.

Threat stories contain the information that formed the original experience of threat, but instead of justifying a storyline about being attacked and needing to defend, they hold the data that express parties' desires, needs, values, and identity that insight mediators know as parties' cares. They are the stories that explain what matters to parties, and how what matters is being experienced as something that needs to be protected. Stories about threats-to-cares are rarely shared between conflicting parties, and if they are shared they are seldom heard by others involved in the conflict because these individuals have their minds turned to protecting what matters to them. But threats-to-care stories hold the potential for parties to gain new insight about their interactions. When they begin to understand each other differently, they access new ways of interpreting actions and intentions, empowering them to seek less conflictual ways of interacting with each other.

In Chapter Six I examine many of the strategies and skills that insight mediators use to help parties shift from rehashing their defend stories to bringing their threat stories to light. Experienced mediators who are not familiar with insight mediation might at first be confused about what is really different, since insight mediators use some of the same communication skills and conflict strategies employed in other forms of mediation, including active listening, paraphrasing, open questions, and being elicitive, rather than directive.[5] Although the differences in approach might appear subtle, they are significant in terms of effect. Here is how.

---

5 See, for instance, Bishop et al. (2015, chap. 5); and Moore (2003).

Selective use of paraphrasing

First, as insight mediation has evolved, the use of paraphrasing – which includes rephrasing, rewording, reflecting, or restating what a party has just said – has become more and more selective. Selectivity serves the purpose of ensuring that the threats to an individual's cares are brought to the surface and understood. To facilitate this, an insight mediator intentionally does not paraphrase the "defend" content of defend stories, or does so only minimally. Instead, the mediator will concentrate on paraphrasing non-defensive communication exchanges to ensure understanding.

Not paraphrasing defend narratives is particularly noticeable early on in the mediation process, when parties almost always begin by speaking about all the reasons they believe their actions are justified, why they are right, and how they feel victimized. Much of this way of talking is an attempt, either conscious or unconscious, to get the mediator on that party's side or to generate empathy for the difficulty of the situation the party has been experiencing. Sometimes it is because that is what the mediator asked the party to talk about through such open questions as: "What is the problem?" "What has been happening?" "What are the issues here?" Not only are insight mediators careful not to restate defend narratives; they deliberately do not ask parties in the opening phases to talk about the conflict situation, but ask them instead to talk about their hopes for change. I elaborate on this point shortly, but first I want to make it clear that I am not saying that parties' defend stories contain irrelevant or unimportant information that does not need to be discussed in the mediation; rather, there is a better way and a better time to bring this information to the surface and engage with it. Paraphrasing the content that justifies a person's actions is sure to block or increase resistance to learning by the other party. This is because defend stories tend to blame and judge others. Feeling wrongly judged and blamed escalates existing negative feelings and thoughts. Insight mediators do not ask about problems, issues, or solutions early in the mediation, since doing so tends to close off, rather than to open up, opportunities for the parties to talk about what really matters to them.

The hope question

Second, at the beginning of the mediation, the insight mediator intentionally opens pathways for learning to occur. Instead of asking the parties to talk about the conflict, the mediator asks them to begin by talking about how they imagine a successful conversation today will better their lives tomorrow. It is a "hope" question that deliberately avoids asking for details about issues or what it is that the parties want. Rather than starting the conversation by focusing on problems, the opening question invites the parties to talk about their hopes by asking them to imagine how being able to engage in dialogue will improve their situation. It is a question about interpersonal relations, rather than about individual or shared interests, and it aims to bring to the surface the parties' higher-level values and motivations for being in mediation. Doing so elicits information unlikely to have been part of the conflict dialogue thus far. This new information opens a pathway for a mediator to explore something other than the party's defend narrative that is sure to convey judgment and blame. It moves the conversation from accusation towards what is valued.

Hope questions are often a surprise to the parties, since they tend to shift the parties from a position of "defending one's corner" to one of being hopeful. The expression of hope is meaningful to other parties because it lacks judgment and blame. When asked, "What are you hoping will be better in your life after talking to each other today?" it is common for parties to express the hope for a better relationship, a less stressful environment, a happier household, a more peaceful neighbourhood, a more prosperous business, and so on. It is from this place of hope that the mediator begins to bring to surface blockages to the realization of these hopes. All too often, however, a party will respond to the hope question with judgment or blame, and the mediator needs to notice this and continue to pursue a line of response that elicits values. I explore how this is done in the explanation of phase two of insight mediation in Chapter Four. Opening a pathway to achieving the parties' hopes is the quintessence of an insight mediation session.

Noticing defend responses

A third action to minimize defend conversations between the parties is to notice when parties are responding defensively. If, for instance, the mediator notices that the parties are quarrelling, convincing, persuading, or becoming more closed and less curious, he or she does not paraphrase what has just been said, but instead will ask an open, curious question about what lies beneath the defend response as a way to begin to bring the threat story to the surface.

To give an example, rather than paraphrase what a party has just said about why she believes she is being unfairly accused of discrimination by the other party, the mediator acknowledges having listened – "the possibility of a discrimination suit is really troubling you" – then asks the party to talk about what it would mean if this were to happen: "What do you fear you would lose if the other party did formalize its accusations?" The question is intended to bring to the surface imagined unwelcome or dire threats to the party's identity or values. Uncovering that threat then gives the mediator a direction for exploring what lies beneath the party's actions: "Your fear of losing your job over something you had no notion of doing is what is keeping you from inviting her to attend group meetings and discussion groups. Talk more about what you were trying to protect when you took that action."

Avoiding asking why

A fourth and fairly straightforward strategy mediators use to avoid unintentionally inviting parties to tell defend stories is to avoid asking them too many questions about actions that were taken, such as: "Why did you do that?" "Why did you not think to tell her?" "Why did you take the compressed work week away?" "Why" questions tend to put the parties on the defensive because they often hear them as judgments and accusations. Avoiding asking too many "why" questions is likely to be a familiar communication strategy to mediators trained in other models as well.

Acting with responsive intentionality

Acting with responsive intentionality is another core principle of the practice of insight mediation that bears mentioning here. Responsive intentionality means that the mediator intervenes with informed intention in response to the parties' words and actions. Insight mediators are diligent about not leading the parties in their story telling or towards solutions, choosing instead to follow them in conversation. Following the parties as they talk is central to the practice of transformative mediation as well (Bush and Folger 2004); yet, although there is overlap between the two practices, there is considerable difference: insight mediators not only follow the conversation, they also explore it, which is contrary to the belief in the transformative model that the mediator should be non-interventionist. Instead, the insight mediator's response is based on his or her knowledge of theory and on his or her experience that helps to predict when a particular intervention will be useful. Whatever response is chosen should stay within the realm of the parties' own storytelling. Moving the conversation towards a different line of inquiry would be considered directive, a strategy that insight mediation does not condone.

Acting with responsive intentionality also means that the mediator does not simply follow prescribed steps, but knowingly and intentionally chooses a communication tool from his or her "tool box" based on what he or she knows about human interaction and conflict. As such, the mediator is responsive and non-directive. Responsive intentionality, as a concept, ensures that the mediator is careful not to take the lead when he or she discovers a way to resolve the conflict. Instead, the mediator lets the parties lead the conversation, and then responds to this conversation with interventions that are theoretically and practically sound and on topic. This is the real core of responsive intentionality: being able to differentiate between cognition of self and other that enables the mediator to facilitate the other's thinking, rather than asking the other to focus on the mediator's thinking.

Take the situation of a party speaking out strongly and in anger about an issue. The insight mediator, drawing on what he or she knows about not attending to strong emotion, responds with a listening skill called "reflecting emotion" (see Chapter Six). This particular skill lets the party know that the *feelings* behind the words were heard: "I can hear from your tone and see from your body language that you are very angry about being accused of discrimination." Not to acknowledge or name the emotion can cause the emotion to escalate and be expressed even more loudly. Because the insight mediator also knows that feelings indicate that a care is threatened, he or she likely follows the acknowledgment of emotion with a curious question aimed at uncovering anticipated threats: "What do you imagine will happen if this suit goes forward?" In responding in this manner, the mediator might reduce or eliminate the strong emotion linked to the threat, as well as open the door to discovering the threat-to-care behind the feeling. Being intentional and responsive by following the party's dialogue using the skills of noticing, listening, and asking a non-judgmental question about what the party has expressed helps the mediator gain insight and thus learn.

Responsive intentionality is about the mediator locating the experiences that evoke the interest and curiosity of the parties. The mediator's questioning is at all times intended to help parties regain their curiosity about each other in order to learn. His or her strategies are focused and intentional; they are responsive to, and in service of, the parties' own lines of interest and curiosity.

The insight mediator learns to respond with intention by reflecting in the moment and silently asking himself or herself: "Why am I using that particular intervention now?" "Why am I acting in the way I am at this moment in time?" "What theory of practice is guiding me?" "What leads me to think that this intervention would be helpful?" Becoming a reflective practitioner is an important feature in most mediation models.[6] As an example of how reflective practice is developed in new mediators, the insight mediation coaching community at Carleton University asks learners in debriefing sessions such questions as: "Why did you choose that particular strategy at that particular moment in the mediation?" "What happened when they intervened in that way?" "How useful was that particular intervention?" "How did you know it was useful?" "What might you do differently knowing what you know now?" The coaches also ask the role-players to respond to a similar question after the mediator has explained his or her viewpoint, as a way to verify how helpful that intervention was to the person playing the role of the party. Learning to reflect both "in action" and "on action" are key ingredients for good mediation practice, which is why reflective practice is common to many mediation styles. In insight mediation it is the recognition that people can come up with their own solutions when they are thinking more optimally – in other words, when they are not cognitively constricted by threat – that makes reflective practice and responsive intentionality essential components of the insight mediator's work.

---

6 See, for instance, Lang and Taylor (2000); and Schon (1983).

Chapter Three

Interaction and Insight:
The Learning Theory underlying Insight
Mediation Practice

In this chapter I answer some common questions about insight mediation: What theory informs insight mediation practice? What is the difference when the mediator intervenes in a conflict using a learning
perspective instead of a problem-solving approach? How does the role
of facilitating learning between conflicting parties influence how the
insight mediator does his or her work? How does this differ from how
mediators trained in other approaches do theirs? To answer these and
other questions requires an explanation of aspects of Lonergan's ([1957]
1992) theory of learning and insight, since insight theory is foundational to the practice of insight mediation. More recently, however, other
social and psychological theories have helped to explain and support
the practice of insight mediation, so I will also touched upon them.[1]

I begin the discussion with an explanation of Lonergan's four operations of learning: experience, understanding, judgment, and decision.
This is followed by a discussion of a number of insight mediation practices that stand out as somewhat distinct. They include asking about
hopes, noticing defend patterns of interaction, deepening understanding of threats-to-cares, recognizing feelings as carriers of value, and distinguishing between levels of value. The chapter concludes with a

---

1 See, for instance, Sargent, Picard, and Jull (2011), who show how the insight approach
helps us to think about conflict differently. A particularly powerful examination of the
insight method is Price (2013). Based on his examination of John Burton's (1990a,b)
work on human needs theory and conflict, Price argues that using the insight approach to conflict analysis offers a way of overcoming the shortcomings of Burton's
approach to explaining conflict (2013, 109).

discussion of how a relational view of social action has influenced not only the development of insight mediation, but also the transformative (Bush and Folger 2004) and narrative mediation (Winslade and Monk 2000) models. To illustrate how world views influence practice, I contrast insight mediation with key ideas about interest-based mediation (Fisher and Ury 1981), an approach that focuses on solving the problem from a liberal, rational, and individualist perspective. I also contrast insight mediation with aspects of narrative and transformative mediation models.

Insight Mediation and Learning

Recall that insight mediation began with a series of questions: What are the parties doing when they lock themselves in conflict? Why is it so difficult for the parties to resolve these conflicts on their own? How can conflict practitioners best help individuals and groups embroiled in conflict? And, more specifically, how can mediators be better at their work? As these questions began to be answered, insight researchers focused attention on how mediators can help empower conflicting parties to engage in dialogue that will help them discover less threatening ways of interacting with each other.

This work has led insight mediation advocates to conclude that the transformation that empowers parties to better their conflict situation happens through learning. Thus, the primary goal of an insight mediator is to open the doors to learning. Helping conflicting parties learn more about themselves and each other as part of the conflict dynamic guides the interventions of the insight practitioner. Changing how a conflict is understood can change one or more of the variables contributing to the conflict – changes that, in turn, can lead to changes in conflict behaviour (Price 2013, 120).

Thinking about conflict intervention as a learning endeavour is not to suggest that, in insight mediation, solving problems or reaching agreement is unimportant – of course, they matter – but the way to solve problems and settle issues in dispute is through the process of learning something new. The role of the mediator is to help the parties create a learning environment in which they are able to talk about what is threatening what matters to them. In this way, the parties discover ways of interacting that are less threatening, thus reducing the need to continue the defend interactions that are sustaining the conflict. Sometimes this means that the conflict is fully resolved. Other times it means that the conflicting parties find acceptable ways of living with their differences. It is possible to find safer and more peaceful ways of interacting even when the threats are real and cannot be fully eliminated. Insight mediation does not promise a miraculous cessation or final resolution of conflict – unfortunately, life does not generally work that way. It does, however, offer the possibility of dialogue, which in itself can bring welcome change to an ongoing and difficult situation. Furthermore, the way we learn to approach conflict today is thought to affect positively how we respond to conflict tomorrow.

Learning how our actions and the actions of others can create and sustain conflict provides insight on how we might respond differently in a similar situation in the future. Understanding more about our values and how they can differ from those of other people makes us better able to react differently to what is going on around us. Changing our actions can change how others act. It is these changed interactions that offer the possibility that our differing cares can coexist without the necessity of conflict. This is why changes brought about through learning can be so powerful and so lasting.

Learning, then, is a critical component of constructive dialogue and therefore of insight mediation. So, what exactly does learning mean? To be sure, learning is a process that involves more than the passive reception of information. As a process it is nonlinear and ongoing. Learning is about answering questions that engage us in four very distinct operations: 1) experiencing and noticing; 2) understanding and insight; 3) judging and verifying; and 4) valuing and deciding (Melchin and Picard 2008). Figure 4 illustrates the four operations of learning.

These four operations of learning take place in each and every one of us as we seek to understand our day-to-day world. Mostly they go unnoticed. They are a part of an innate curiosity to understand our own selves along with the people and events we encounter. Insight occurs when our curiosity hits upon the answer to our questions – insight that can be experienced in powerful and affective ways. During the mediation session, both the parties and the mediator learn, and this learning can change how they see things and how they act.

Here is a simple and personal illustration of the four operations at work. I awake Saturday morning with the whole day ahead of me. It is a beautiful sunny spring day, and I just want to stay in bed and bask in it, perhaps even give myself over to reading a novel. My pragmatic side says, you had better get moving and not waste away the day. So I ponder the question, what will I do? I know that I need to work on

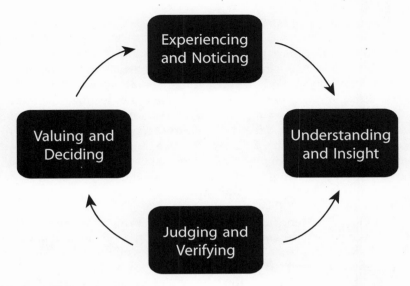

Figure 4: Operations of Learning

completing this book. My "experience" knows that I am quite capable of taking the day and accomplishing very little. I really do not want to do that today, as I have a deadline to meet. So I ask myself, what do I need to accomplish today to feel good? I start making a list. I ask my husband his thoughts on organizing the day. By expanding my "data of experience" (Lonergan's operation 1), I am able to move on to operation 2, "understanding." My husband offers to take on some of the chores on my list, suggesting that I write in the morning and then take the afternoon to relax or go for a walk with him. This makes me happy, and I realize that I was looking for support and maybe even a little sympathy because I needed to work on a Saturday. I have just experienced a direct insight that broadens my understanding of what is important to me. Now that I better understand my earlier procrastination, I "verify" (operation 3) that my husband is willing to tackle the laundry and the grocery shopping. I return to my question – what will I do? – with much more enthusiasm. I take responsibility for my actions by sitting down at my computer and starting to work. I have "decided" (operation 4) that I will work until around one o'clock, then put the book writing aside and take my husband for a walk to the local market.

The four operations of learning

1. EXPERIENCING AND NOTICING

"Experiencing and noticing" is about getting the data for the operations of understanding and judgment. Getting the data requires that we immerse ourselves in experiences of seeing, hearing, feeling, imagining, and remembering. It requires that we notice, and question, what we see, hear, taste, smell, and feel. But before we can ask what these experiences and data are about, we need to notice them by ensuring that we pay close attention. With this in mind, insight mediation has developed the core skill of "noticing" to help mediators remember to pay close attention to the parties' actions and words, almost as if they are in awe of them. I explain this skill later in the chapter.

Of course, experiencing something and acquiring more information about it is not the same as truly understanding the information or experience. Never is this truer than in conflict. Parties might hear what other parties are saying and see what they are doing, but at times they will be confused by what is said, or totally misunderstand what others mean by their words and actions. Misinterpreting or misunderstanding others' intentions is at the root of many conflicts because when those involved respond to each other in ways that appear potentially harmful or, at the very least, do not make sense, the situation tends to manifest into outright conflict.

2. UNDERSTANDING AND INSIGHT

The desire to make sense of others' actions and our own experiences occurs at the second level of learning: "understanding." Understanding is when insight occurs – insight that answers our questions or sets our questioning on a new track. Insight occurs in minds that are wondering, and it is the act of wondering that generates the curiosity needed to begin asking questions. Wanting to understand is about finding answers to the question, what is it? The answer to this question is insight. Before the insight, we cannot imagine the answer to our question; after the insight, we can neither imagine nor remember our inability to understand (Melchin and Picard 2008, 55).

We have all experienced having an insight; it is not something that is unfamiliar. Insight involves that sudden moment of clarity, that "aha" moment when the light bulb suddenly goes on and we hit on the answer to a question that has been eluding us – the moment when we shift from being confused to suddenly becoming brilliant. Insight happens quite unexpectedly. It comes to a mind that is ready to receive it – a mind that is wondering, questioning, and wanting to understand. Once we have an insight, we can never go back to our original state of not knowing. The experience is both cognitive and physical, and it brings about a change in us that is lasting. Insight yields direction and decisions to be acted upon. Insight changes not only how we view things, but also how we feel about them, and reshapes the way we experience sensory data the next time around. Knowing that there are times when learning can occur suddenly and at a deep level helps to make sense of what mediators commonly refer to as the "magic of mediation."

In mediation, achieving insight is all about asking questions that open up new lines of curiosity and inquiry. Becoming more curious about oneself and about others is at the heart of the learning process in insight mediation. Insight can come in two ways: as a direct insight or as a reverse insight.

Direct insight. Insight that brings together and integrates our data of experience is known as "direct insight." Direct insight keeps us on our current path of inquiry, and at times can be experienced as an "aha" moment. In my previous example, I have a direct insight when I learn my husband is willing to take on some of the household chores as way to support my need to do some writing while also having some time to relax and be with him. In another example, I have a direct insight after following the directions to a new meeting room and, to my delight, I discover a wonderful location across campus in which to hold small training workshops. Direct insight can occur gradually over time, or it can come suddenly and when we least expect it. Either way, it is total, affecting both what we think and how we feel. In mediation, for example, a supervisor learns that one of his employees is resisting the new system of accounting, not because she is reluctant, but because layoffs followed the implementation of new systems in the past. Her refusal even to discuss the new system idea now makes sense, and the supervisor can respond to her fears in a more productive way. Gaining this knowledge is a direct insight.

Reverse insight. Insight that lends itself to questioning the actual learning system is, according to Lonergan, inverse insight. The concept of inverse insight is complex, and there is debate among Lonergan scholars about its meaning. To respect these debates, in insight mediation we use the term "reverse insight" to refer to those times when we move from one line of questioning to another because we suddenly realize that we have been asking about the wrong question altogether. Reverse insight requires that we ask new types of questions and pay attention to different sets of data. Getting the insight that "we can't get there from here" disengages one line of questioning and produces another. Rather than hitting upon a solution, reverse insight recognizes that getting answers requires asking new lines of questions and exploring in new directions.

Reverse insight causes parties to abandon their current line of thinking and take up a new line of questioning that is more relevant for what they are trying to understand. They recognize that they have been barking up the wrong tree, so to speak, and they begin to ask questions about entirely new sets of data. Reverse insight involves a three-step process: 1) a direct insight that provides information and is followed by 2) a judgment that how the information was understood is wrong, and 3) pursuing a new line of curiosity and questioning (Picard and Melchin 2007, 43).

I first came to understand the idea of reverse insight while examining my doctoral research data. I was repeatedly encountering data that made little sense, and I was struggling to refine my coding scheme so it would uncover answers to the questions I was asking. When discussing this problem with my research committee, it was suggested that the questions I was asking of the data might be wrong and that I should "take a step back and let the data speak to me." Shifting my focus from looking for how similar patterns from respondents' meaning making answered my questions to looking for what their responses were not telling me about my hypothesis altered my frame of reference, and in no time at all the focus of my research was changed. It was not just that new information had been produced, but that the line of intelligibility I had been pursuing no longer made sense, and the new line of inquiry seemed so obvious that it was hard to believe I had not seen it before. A light bulb clearly had gone on for me!

To take a mediation example, reverse insight occurs when a wife comes to understand that her husband is not deliberately trying to make her life difficult and that he really does care about the children. Letting go of her direct insight that his actions were about trying to hurt her allows her to work more easily with him and the mediator on developing a parenting plan.

3. JUDGING AND VERIFYING

Lonergan's third operation of learning, judging and verifying, asks, do I have this right? In answering this question, insight mediators use a skill called "verifying" to confirm that both they and the parties have in fact understood correctly. I examine this skill in Chapter Six. Verifying understanding and meaning making that produces direct insight encourages the parties to continue down the road of trying to understand each other. Verifying that detaches the parties from dead end lines of inquiry (reverse insight) enables the parties to leave the path they were on and move onto a new line of inquiry. Mediators engage in a different type of discovery process when they verify whether direct or reverse insight is correct. Conceptually they wonder, Is what I think I now understand actually correct? Have I missed something of importance? Is there something more to know? The goal of verifying is not to evaluate what we know, but to confirm whether our understanding of the narratives and normative social relations carried by our feelings has been correctly understood. It asks the proverbial question, is it so? Continuing with my earlier example of thinking that I have discovered a new meeting space, I check with the administrator of this new room to see if people from other faculties may book it. When I learn that, in fact, I may do so, I move to the fourth operation of learning, which involves considering once more the value of using the space for the coaches workshop and deciding to call and see if it is available when I need it.

4. VALUING AND DECIDING

The fourth operation, valuing and deciding, is where we make decisions based on the importance we place on our new understanding; we then act based on our valuing. Valuing involves reflecting on whether or not to follow through on our operations of understanding and judgment, while deciding involves determining how to take responsibility for our actions. In recognition of the significance of what we now understand, the operation asks the question, so what? We value, decide, and then act. In mediation we see these decisions occurring in various ways – for instance, when parties own up to their mistakes, offer or accept apologies, and decide to act in ways that are less threatening to others. In my workshop space example, after thinking about it further and determining it would be a great meeting space (the operation of valuing) and that it is available, I call (the operation of deciding) to book it for a coaches training session next month.

It is important to emphasize that deciding does not always follow directly from the operation of judgment. We reach decisions only after returning to get new insight into possible courses of action, verifying their value, then choosing how to take responsibility for acting. The process of learning is not linear. It involves looping back from the operation of decision and action to the operations of experience, understanding, and judgment, then back to decision and action, then back again to experience, understanding, judgment, and so forth, in a continuous loop.[2] Learning is thus a continual cycle. There might be times when we are cognizant of these operations, but most often they happen in the background of our consciousness.

Insight mediation is a process of learning. The parties learn about what drives their actions, possibly as a way to change them. Mediators continually engage in learning about, making sense of, and verifying what the parties are saying, feeling, and valuing. In addition, mediators pay attention to how their actions and the actions of others in the room are affecting those present. In particular, they notice if the parties' interactions are advancing the conversation or closing it off, and if the latter, they ask themselves what intervention might put the conversation on a better path. Insight mediators are also trained to notice what is happening within themselves, paying particular attention to what might be negatively affecting their attentiveness and helpfulness. Continual reflection while things are going on and after the fact facilitates the learning process for both the parties and the mediator.

Let's look at some of the practices of insight mediators that, because they use a process of learning to change conflict situations, can be considered distinct.

Insight Mediation Practices that Stand out as Distinct

Five insight mediation practices appear to be distinct from what mediators trained in other mediation models do: 1) noticing patterns of interaction, especially defend patterns; 2) deepening the understanding of threats; 3) recognizing feelings as carriers of values; 4) distinguishing between hierarchical levels of value; and 5) beginning the mediation by asking about hopes, rather than issues.

---

2 Drawing on Lonergan, Price (2013, 118) explains conflict behaviour as engaging individuals in an even more complex pattern of human consciousness that involves not only the reflective levels of experiencing, understanding, and verifying, but also an existential level of valuing, deliberating, and evaluating that leads to decision and action.

1. Noticing patterns of interaction, especially defend patterns

Insight mediators are taught to "notice" what is happening around them. As a practice, noticing involves paying close attention to all verbal and non-verbal exchanges within the mediation. It involves observing the parties' interactions to discover their pattern of interaction with each other and how these patterns might be interfering with the parties' ability to resolve the conflict situation on their own. Noticing expands the mediator's knowledge and understanding, which, in turn, influences the mediator's actions. Noticing is all about the mediator learning.

As a skill, noticing involves two distinct actions. First, mediators ensure that they pay close attention, that they are fully present, that they are listening, and that they have cleared their minds of their own paraphernalia as much as possible in order to be open to what is going on around them. Second, mediators tell others what they are noticing. This allows mediators to verify that the picture that has formed in their minds is similar to what the parties understand or intend. It also helps the parties to learn how their words and actions are being interpreted and if they are communicating the message they intend. Discovering how others are interpreting our words or actions allows for the possibility of adjusting them.

2. Deepening the conversation on threats

Deepening conversations are aimed at bringing the parties' threats-to-cares to the surface. This emphasis is consistent with the insight mediator's understanding that conflict arises from the experience that one party's actions threatens the other party's cares, creating defend patterns of interaction that sustain the conflict. Deepening conversations help the parties discover if their differing cares can coexist without threat. Noticing how the parties' communication patterns contribute to existing threat narratives and defend patterns of interaction is a key function of the insight mediator.

Deepening the conversation on threats-to-cares can also involve the mediator asking the parties to talk about what they expected the other would have done differently if it were true that the other really was not trying to cause harm – in other words, asking about a second-level value, which I explain shortly. Individuals often judge others' behaviour not so much by what they do, as by what they do not do, so discovering this can be useful. The mediator also asks the parties to talk about what the others' actions would need to look like for them not to feel so threatened. This is not an outcome or problem-solving question, but an elicitive question that tries to uncover normative patterns of cooperation – for instance, what it looks like to be a good neighbour, good co-worker, good manager, good parent, good friend, and so forth. Through deepening conversations, the mediator helps to generate new insight about how the parties' interactions are threatening to each other and, when the threats occur, about not only changing how the problem is viewed, but, often more important, altering how the parties feel about each other.

3. Recognizing feelings as carriers of values

Feelings point to values. In conflict, feelings play a significant role in both the creation and the unravelling of the situation. Differing values might produce similar feelings for diverse reasons. For this reason insight mediators need to surface, manage, and explore what the parties' feelings are about. They do this by noticing, acknowledging, and normalizing feelings, and by inviting the parties to express their feelings and the reasons they hold them. Knowing that the feelings of conflicting parties are the pathways to discovering their cares and the threats-to-cares is thought to be the key to producing change. Insight mediation's approach to feelings thus differs from approaches that tend to suppress feelings because they can interfere with the settlement process.

Along with a heightened sense of noticing feelings, insight mediators ask elicitive questions that help the parties identify their feelings and their source. Returning to our example of the employee who is resisting the new accounting method, the mediator might say: "You clearly reject the offer of additional training. When she talks about training as one option, how does the team feel? Where does the fear about losing jobs come from, and why you are so certain that is what is going to happen in this instance? Has something happened in the past that leads you to that conclusion, and if so, what was it?"

Insight practitioners are aware not only that feelings are connected to values, but also that feelings are connected to past experiences and to imagined futures that hold unwelcome, if not dire, consequences. For this reason they query what is going on in the present in relation to past experiences and anticipated futures. Linking these events and delinking incorrect links are insight skills that I discuss in Chapter Six.

4. Distinguishing between hierarchical levels of values

Through Lonergan insight mediators have come to understand that human beings are motivated by three hierarchical levels of values (Melchin and Picard 2008, 70–4): 1) personal goals, desires, interests, and human needs; 2) expected and normative patterns of relations; and 3) judgments about the progress or decline of society.

First-level values involve goods that we desire and need at the individual level. Maslow's hierarchy of needs[3] and Fisher and Ury's (1991) concept of interests both reside at this level. Examples of first-level values include winning a sports competition, getting a raise or receiving some other form of recognition for doing a good job, or setting a goal for losing weight and achieving it.

Second-level values involve "normative and expected patterns of interaction": relationships, institutions, and forms of social cooperation whereby we join with others to provide the things that, as individuals, we desire and need. These cooperative relationships involve goals and obligations that none of us might desire individually, but that we all depend on to meet the needs of all. We do not always formulate these goods or obligations explicitly, but they are often carried in our feelings – feelings about loyalty, fidelity, job satisfaction, professional responsibility, parenting, friendship, and so forth. At this second level of values, we take social relationships and institutions as they are; we accept them, their goals and obligations. Second-level values make room for mediators to try to make sense of parties' actions and decisions that might be confusing because they are not necessarily self-focused.

Third-level values involve a critical assessment of second-level values, as they are what hold meaning and purpose in our social world. In other words, it is at this third level that we scrutinize our social relationships and institutions by asking questions about justice, human rights, respect for human dignity, oppression, and unfair social structures and practices. This level of critical scrutiny gives rise to the larger values that start making claims about the meaning of life. At this level, we have strong feelings not only about the social institutions that exist,

---

3 Abraham Maslow, in his 1943 paper, "A Theory of Human Motivation," used the terms "physiological," "safety," "belongingness," "love," "esteem," "self-actualization," and "self-transcendence" to describe human motivations; see also Maslow (1954).

but also about those we want to bring into existence through our decisions and actions.

Levels of value are interconnected and hierarchical. For instance, we will relinquish first-level needs and interests to retain second level co-operative patterns of social relations: we will give in to the choices of our children, for example, even though we disagree with them, in order to build relations and maintain harmony in the family. At other times we forgo personal relations in favour of what we believe to be in the best interests of society, a higher-level value. This is what motivates men and women to decide to leave their families and the safety of their community and go to war. Understanding that higher levels of values are at work in our decision making helps to explain why parties act in ways that at first glance appear to go against their self-interest and needs.

Each of these three levels of values can operate in conflict. Helping conflicting parties to recognize what level, or levels, of values are being threatened can motivate them to search for new ways of interacting that will protect, rather than threaten, these values. Although insight mediators agree with other approaches about not "trading" on values, they do not agree that values have no place "at the table." Rather, insight mediators believe that developing a deeper understanding of the values at play in conflict is the only route to discovering non-threatening ways of interacting. Interest-based practitioners are generally leery of discussing values in the mediation session because of the view that values are non-negotiable. They understand their role as facilitating negotiation, which means avoiding information that could negatively influence the negotiation process. For the same reason, they also discourage the presence of strong feelings in mediation since they might interfere with reaching a settlement. In the insight approach, in contrast, feelings and values are viewed as important data to be identified and understood, as it is only by revealing them that the threats that gave rise to the conflict can be reduced or eliminated. Values and feelings, as well as interests and needs, helped to create the conflict, and for that reason they cannot be set apart from the mediation encounter.

Insight mediators are trained to deepen the conversation as a way to help the parties gain insight into things they had not necessarily realized they valued so strongly. Understanding that there is a three-level structure to values gives mediators a range of opportunities to facilitate discussions about values. Such discussions quite often involve inquiry at the second level of values because, as human beings, we take patterns of cooperation for granted and assume others hold similar values, so we rarely talk openly about them. Although it might be relatively easy for the parties to articulate their personal goals and interests (first-level values), they often have difficulty articulating the goals and obligations embedded in their day-to-day relations and social patterns of cooperation.

Gaining insight into our values also allows others to understand them. Learning how values influence decisions empowers the parties to make different decisions by delinking threats through the three-step process of: 1) gaining insight into what we and others really care about (a direct insight); 2) realizing that prior assumptions about the other party's motivations are wrong (a reverse insight); and 3) evoking a new line of curiosity about others and their relationship to us.

5. Asking about hopes, rather than about issues, at the start of mediation

In the previous chapter I discussed the practice of asking about hopes, rather than about problems and issues, early in the mediation session, but it bears mentioning again. Eliciting hopes is a purposeful strategy to move the parties away from defend narratives from the outset. It is important because one party's defend story will perpetuate another's defend response, creating a defend pattern of interaction right at the beginning of the mediation that pretty much closes off the possibility that the parties will learn anything new about each other. It makes sense, then, that the mediator will want to minimize defend responses to prevent exacerbating the parties' intransigence. Knowing this, the insight mediator begins by asking each party to talk about his or her hopes for a better tomorrow if the mediation is successful. The question sounds something like this: "If you are able to talk to each other today, how are you hoping that will improve your interactions at work?" "How do you hope working through your differences today will make things better for you tomorrow?" "What do you hope will be better tomorrow if you can talk about what really matters to each of you today?"

Asking about hopes is inviting the parties to talk about what motivated them to come to mediation. In this instance, it is fair to assume that the motivation elicited will be stronger than the negative experience likely anticipated by sitting across from someone in mediation. Parties come to mediation seeking constructive change. Seldom, however, is this motive clear in a person's mind, and it takes a few tries to elicit a statement of hope, rather than one of accusation or demand. In addition, parties come to mediation prepared to defend their case, so they can be taken aback when they are asked about hopes for a better tomorrow. For this reason they often need to be asked the question a few times and to be given time to think about how to answer.

The point of the hope question is to begin changing how the parties talk to each other. Discovering that the person you are in conflict with has a similar hope can begin to make room for listening and learning. Because this information is generally new and non-accusatory, there is no need to defend from it. The discussion of hopes also gives the mediator a way to create a new narrative that explores the parties' experiences, understandings, judgments, and decision making in less threatening ways. Questioning what can be done in the mediation to achieve each party's hopes lets the mediator stay clear of inadvertently inviting the parties to speak about their justifications for being "right," thus setting off their defend narratives.

Insight mediators' use of the hope question to change the parties' patterns of interaction is somewhat similar to the focus of other mediators on interests, rather than on positions (Fisher and Ury 1991) in that both strategies aim to change conflict behaviour that is unhelpful. On that note, let's move on to examine other similarities and differences between insight mediation and other approaches.

The Influence of a Relational View on Mediation Practices

Questions such as these are sometimes asked about insight mediation: Is insight mediation really different? Is it not just another form of what mediators already do? Why do we need another approach to mediation? Can I sometimes be an insight mediator and at other times be an interest-based, transformative, or narrative mediator? Doesn't my choice of approach depend on the parties and what they want, rather than on how I was trained?

These questions are complex, and not easily answered, and the answers are not necessarily easy for mediation practitioners to accept. The notion that there are new ideas that challenge current understandings can lead experienced mediators to question their practice. For the most part this is good, but ideas that tug at the roots of mediators' identities might cause them to stand firm upon the ground they know and become closed-minded. Defending what is known to protect one's sense of self worth inhibits change, but new knowledge and change are needed to advance mediation as a profession.

Contemporary models of mediation, including transformative (Bush and Folger 2004), narrative (Winslade and Monk 2000), and insight, are embedded in a relational world view of human action. This view differs from the individualist perspective that undergirds the interest-based approach for dealing with conflict (Fisher and Ury 1981). Individualist and relational viewpoints are social theories that have long engaged philosophers in academic debate. These are the theories that shape our social, political, and legal institutions because they hold basic assumptions about social interactions that influence how we act. It is from these broad social theories that theories about conflict are formed. And it is from theories of conflict that the roles and actions of mediators are based. Figure 5 depicts the theories of conflict and human action that inform insight mediation.

The relational world view

The relational view emerged from thinkers who posited a communitarian social philosophy such as Charles Taylor (1989, 1992), who drew upon Aristotle to criticize views of individualism in liberal philosophy, Robert Bellah et al. (1986), Amitai Etzioni (1993), Alasdair MacIntyre (1981), and Michael Sandel (1982). In all three approaches to mediation (insight, transformative, and narrative), the mediator engages with conflicting parties on the understanding that they are connected to each other by cultures, traditions, religions, communities, and relationships.

Relational social theory conceives of human beings as social actors responding to their environment. We live in networks of relationships that are meaningful to us and help us to form our identity. We are conscious of how others respond to us, and we relate to them in ways that generate and reinforce our identity and how we want others to think of us. Our actions are designed not only to realize goals and meet interests, but also to influence how others perceive and respond to us. We are more than self-interested thinkers – we are reflexive. Acting relationally involves promoting relationships; pursuing interests alone often excludes the pursuit of relationships. How we act reflects how we participate in relationships and our patterns of cooperation with others; it matters that we have good relationships with others. This is why insight mediators understand their role as helping parties to gain more insight into their relations with others.

The relational approach to mediation does not mean that mediation involves only those conflicts that are about relationships. Rather, it refers to the idea that people act in relation to each other and to their

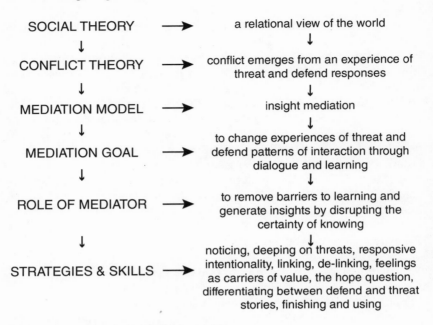

SOCIAL THEORY ⟶ a relational view of the world

CONFLICT THEORY ⟶ conflict emerges from an experience of threat and defend responses

MEDIATION MODEL ⟶ insight mediation

MEDIATION GOAL ⟶ to change experiences of threat and defend patterns of interaction through dialogue and learning

ROLE OF MEDIATOR ⟶ to remove barriers to learning and generate insights by disrupting the certainty of knowing

STRATEGIES & SKILLS ⟶ noticing, deeping on threats, responsive intentionality, linking, de-linking, feelings as carriers of value, the hope question, differentiating between defend and threat stories, finishing and using

Figure 5: Linking Insight Mediation to Theory

environment and not merely on the basis of self-interest or rational choice alone. It means that people are influenced by others and that they influence others even when they do not intend to do so; often they are unaware this has even happened.

Actions are not only purposeful; they are also responsive (Sargent, Picard, and Jull 2011). We not only intend action; we also respond to action. We influence, and are influenced by, our environment. When our environment changes, it influences us in ways we cannot always predict. Our actions are not always calculated, nor are they always in our best interest. Sometimes we act in response to how we *think* others think we should act, rather than how we actually believe we should react. We live in relation to others, not separate and apart from them. When we are purposeful, often our purpose is to promote interpersonal relations with others. This purpose is itself relational, and involves interpreting others' actions, understanding our relationships with them, and responding in terms of our understanding of this relationship.

Relational also means that everything that happens today influences what happens, or does not happen, tomorrow. The "me" who acts as an individual is connected to the "me" whose past relationships have shaped the feelings and expectations that are now the "me" who is acting in the present. How we deal with conflict today affects how we will act in future conflicts. Decisions we make to resolve conflict today influence what we will do tomorrow. What we learn today has consequences for tomorrow. How a problem is solved affect not only us, but those around us – even those we have yet to meet. This is the relational view, and one that is in contrast to the individualist world view.

The individualist world view

Individualist thinkers such as Thomas Hobbes and Niccolò Machiavelli regarded human beings as fundamentally self-referential. This means that our needs and desires are generated internally; we are the authors of our own destiny, so to speak. We are rational decision makers who can pursue our individual interests. To understand conflict, from this perspective, is to understand the individual's interests and needs, for these are what motivate that person's actions.

The interest-based approach to conflict formulated by Roger Fisher and William Ury in *Getting to Yes* (1981) exemplifies conflict as viewed from the individualist perspective. In this approach, conflict is defined as a struggle over the perceived incompatibility of one's goals, needs, and interests with those of others. The focus of mediation is on reaching agreements that settle disputes and solve problems. Reaching agreements in which there is a win-win outcome is the ultimate goal, and this will happen when the parties in conflict focus on their needs and interests, rather than on their positions and demands. Focusing on interests allows more than one solution to the problem to emerge, which, metaphorically speaking "expands the pie." New ways of compromising or collaborating can be found, allowing the parties to save face and meet their needs.

The interest-based approach to conflict is also rooted in a liberal philosophy associated with the work of Rawls (1971) and Dworkin (1977), in which the goal of a democratic society is to maximize freedom and equality for all individuals. Interest-based mediators engage the parties in creatively generating options that meet everyone's interests through strategies that foster collaboration and compromise.

The interest-based approach is widely used and highly valued in contemporary society. It has been shown to be a more efficient, cost-effective, and satisfactory way to deal with disputes that might otherwise be dealt with in a court of law or other social institution (Macfarlane

1995). Given the prevalence of interest-based negotiations and mediation, it is useful to identify how the insight approach differs from the interest-based approach. Below are some basic elements that distinguish the two models. Intertwined in this discussion are also some differences between insight mediation and narrative and transformative models.

Differentiating between Insight and Other Models of Mediation

Before discussing how insight mediation differs from other mediation models, it bears noting that most mediation models follow a similar progression that begins with the parties talking about the nature of the conflict, discussing the impact of the situation and how it might be changed, and concluding with decisions about how those changes can be made by mutual consent. Most models are consensual in that the parties have the choice to participate, and the parties themselves design any solutions reached. Most involve the parties in some form of pre-mediation session to determine their willingness and ability to participate along with determining the appropriateness of the dispute for mediation, and most involve some form of post-mediation follow-up.

Whether insight mediation is truly a new model or simply offers a more comprehensive explanation of what is going on in other mediation models is still unclear in some people's minds. Most agree, however, that distinct features differentiate insight mediation from other practices. These features reflect insight mediation's interpretive and interactionist view of human action and conflict (Sargent, Picard, and Jull 2011), and that it attends to individual cognition within complex social contexts (Price 2013). The extent of these differences is only beginning to be understood. As we continue to investigate the use of insight mediation in a broader range of disputes and with larger groups of people, more differences are sure to be noticed. I touch upon the promise of the expanded use of the insight approach in the final chapter. One point I want to make now is that, by focusing on change brought about through learning, rather than through imposed decision making, promises to make positive and lasting change more possible.

One way to contrast interest-based mediation with insight mediation is to use Fisher and Ury's (1981) four principles of interest-based negotiation. These principles state that a good negotiator and mediator should: 1) separate the people from the problem; 2) focus on interests, not positions; 3) generate options for mutual gain; and 4) use objective criteria.

Separating people from the problem assumes that humans are rational and act independently of one another. This view is in contrast to the insight approach, which regards people as connected to one another and as acting in response to one another. It posits that what we do is not so much an "intended" response as it is a response to our "interpretation" of another's intent. One practical application of this difference is that interest-based practitioners respond to a party's interpretation of intended harm by "reframing" the situation more positively. The insight mediator, in contrast, "deepens" on the threat of intended harm to see whether the threat-to-care, of necessity, must be an ongoing part of the parties' interactions.

Focusing on interests in insight mediation is only a small part of the process. Interests are a lower-level value, and the insight mediator is attentive to noticing, exploring, and surfacing higher-level values that might supersede those at the lower level. These higher-level values involve normative patterns of cooperation, along with judgments about social progress. The interest-based practitioner views interests as objective and determinate. We all have them; we just have to find them and satisfy them. Insight mediation would say that interests are not determinate; rather, they emerge, shift, and change throughout the course of the conflict, and even within the mediation process itself. Discovering common interests and using them as the building blocks to reach solutions is a common interest-based strategy. The insight practitioner does not do this. Working with interests to the exclusion of exploring threats to higher-level values reveals only a part of the conflict story and runs the risk that future conflict will emerge, since the parties will continue to use existing and problematic patterns of interaction. Problem solving alone is likely to have short-lived results; learning how our actions create threat in others has the potential to change how we act forever.

Generating options for mutual gain by using objective criteria suggests that conflict encounters should be addressed in rational and objective ways. At one level this makes some sense, but when we think about conflicts that are not at the level of self-interest alone, objectivity and rationality might not be the best response. I am thinking here of situations in which conflict is logical and arguably the correct response under the circumstances. For example, a teenager who runs away from home to avoid ongoing abuse is considered delinquent in the eyes of the law, but her actions could also be thought of as sensible in light of the abusive situation. Some scholars view the creation of conflict as an appropriate response from groups in oppressive situations. Laura

Nader (1990), for example, has long raised concerns about attempts to achieve harmony in society, believing that discord is sometimes more favourable because it can provide the impetus for change. Other feminist scholars support this idea through their critique of mediation for women, arguing that mediation runs the risk of further marginalizing them thorough its inability to redress power imbalances between the parties, and because privatizing family disputes neglects broader social issues (see Canada 1998).

Other aspects of insight mediation also distinguish it from other mediation approaches. Some of these differences are linked to insight mediation's emphasis on learning; others have emerged from the use of a practice-to-theory and theory-to-practice research methodology. To exemplify this, and at the risk of overgeneralizing, in a situation in which a party responds with negative high emotion and closed-mindedness, the insight mediator's focus on opening the doors to learning would likely lead him or her to *explore* the behaviour and then *deepen* upon it in order to surface the threats-to-cares that are creating the response. Again at the risk of overgeneralizing, in a similar situation the interest-based trained mediator might be more likely to use the skill of reframing to change the emotional or conceptual state of the upset party, rather than delve too deeply into it, since high emotion is seen as a potential barrier to resolution. The transformative mediator is also unlikely to delve into the response, but for different reasons. He or she most likely would paraphrase with the same intensity what it was the party said as a way to encourage the party to continue his or her storytelling and to respect the mediator's role as non-interventionist. The narrative mediator also likely would not engage in a direct query about the behaviour, but instead would externalize the emotion, then seek to create a new narrative that moved away from what was thought of as the problem-saturated story. Each of these responses could prove beneficial in this situation; the point is that the different actions the mediator takes are based on different theoretical premises.

Let's continue to contrast different mediation practices, keeping in mind that not all mediators trained in the same approach necessarily would act in the same manner in the same context, since who we are as people influences how we act as mediators. The interest-based mediator assumes that the parties are acting out of self-interest, and so personal interests need to be clearly identified; the mediator's task is to help the parties express their interests, then negotiate them. The transformative mediator concentrates on the interactions of the parties in mediation, looking for opportunities to foster empowerment and recognition. The narrative mediator, drawing on social constructionist theory, uses his or her knowledge of cultural norms and history to diminish the cultural influences that restrain the parties' ability to understand each other. The insight mediator assumes that the parties often have little or no idea of the inner threats that are at work on each other or how they are sustaining the conflict. For this reason insight mediation requires the mediator to facilitate discovery and learning about oneself and about the other party, which is why they deepen on the conversation, rather than reframe, paraphrase, or externalize it.

Both interest-based and insight mediators agree that a typical response in conflict is to defend one's position. For interest-based practitioners this response reflects the perception of incompatible goals that block the fulfilment of self-interest. For the insight practitioner the hold-tight response is due to the perception of threat to deep levels of feelings and values. Whereas the interest-based mediator seeks to surface the interests of both parties so they can both be achieved, the insight mediator, knowing there are different and potentially multiple levels of values at work, aims to empower the parties to reveal these values. This is accomplished by helping the parties become curious about each other and, through this curiosity, wonder if each other's values could exist in ways that do not threaten those of the other. These different pursuits result in the interest-based mediator's engaging in problem-solving activities, whereas the insight mediator's activities focus on removing obstacles to learning as a way to resolve problems.

To recap, insight mediation takes the disputing parties through an in-depth exploration of the problem because "they must move through it and beyond it to understand the deeper cares, concerns, values, interests, and feelings that underlie the problem" (Picard and Melchin 2007, 50). Thus, insight mediation is relation centred, not solely problem centred. Narrative and transformative models also focus on the relations between the parties, although they tend to steer the parties away from the problem, rather than more deeply into to it, to get to the deeper relations of the conflict. In do so, the narrative mediator hopes to get the parties into a creative space where they can begin to create alternative narratives in relation to each other, since staying with the problem is thought to be disempowering. This idea is shared by the transformative mediator, who believes that exploring the problem will keep the parties in a conflictual place where neither will feel empowered nor be able to recognize the other. The interest-based mediator sees conflict as a problem to be solved, and for that reason relies on problem-solving methods to help the parties settle their differences. The insight mediator, however, knows that the parties care about resolving their issues, and that empowerment, recognition, and alternative ways of relating to each other are important. To these goals the insight practitioner adds the importance of individual cognition and insight in achieving them.

Insights transform our understanding and our feeling about our concerns, interests, and values, as well as our understanding and feeling about other people's concerns, interests, and values. Helping people understand and acknowledge both themselves and each other transforms interpersonal and social relations – transformations that not only will change their interactions in the present, but also influence their interactions in the future.

Advocates of the insight approach hold that, as societies become more diverse, citizens have an increasing need for skills to negotiate social differences and social change, and this includes negotiating conflict (Melchin and Picard 2008, 127). Understanding that the learning involved in resolving conflict engages us in a set of operations that is significantly more complex than the simple transfer of information offers a new pathway for individuals and groups to pursue the skills that will help them to deal more wisely and creatively with conflicts in everyday life today and in the future. Curiosity about oneself and about others is at the heart of a democratic society. When it becomes blocked or damaged by cynicism and scepticism, conflicts emerge. These conflicts, whether small or large, present challenges for personal relations, justice institutions, and democracy. We all have a part to play in resolving these conflicts. Learning about learning can advance the work of transforming conflict.

Chapter Four

Facilitating Change through Learning: Conducting the Mediation Session

Mediation sessions bring the mediator and the disputing parties together in one or more face-to-face meetings. In insight mediation, the aim of these meetings is to facilitate learning among the parties that will enable them to change their defend patterns of interaction and find less threatening and more peaceful ways of interacting. Insight mediators follow five non-linear progressive phases. This progression is similar to what happens in most models where the mediator takes the parties through storytelling, decision making, and closure, although other approaches might explain this progression using more or less than five stages. In insight mediation, these five phases are called: 1) attend to process; 2) broaden understanding; 3) deepen on insights; 4) explore possibilities; and 5) make decisions. There are times when the mediator and the parties move in a fairly straightforward way through the phases. At other times mediation sessions can involve a more back-and-forth process (see Figure 6).

To help illustrate what goes on in each of the five phases, I use excerpts of dialogue between the mediator and the parties in our case study, "The Straw that Broke the Camel's Back," to point out specific communication skills and conflict-resolution techniques. Further explanation of these communication skills appears in Chapter Six.

Mediation sessions occur after the mediator has determined that the situation is appropriate for mediation and after the parties have agreed to participate. This phase, which I discuss in the next chapter, is referred to as pre-mediation. For now it is sufficient to know that pre-mediation involves one-on-one private sessions with the parties to ensure that mediation is an appropriate process for them to attempt to solve their differences. Pre-mediation allows the mediator to assess whether

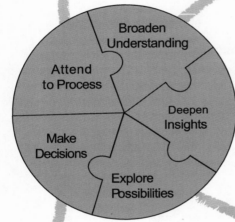

① **Attend to Process**

✓ Develop a shared understanding of the process, ways of interacting, confidentiality, decision making, timeframes, outcome documents
✓ Confirm agreement to proceed
✓ Build rapport

 Broaden Understanding

✓ Begin by identifying hopes: *What do you hope will improve if you can talk today about what really matters to each of you?*
✓ Verify and summarize hopes
✓ Listen for & clarify threats-to- cares
✓ Avoid restating defend stories

 Deepen Insights

✓ Engage in a learning dialogue by discovering & deepening on threats; levels of value & feelings
✓ Discover meaning-making and interpretations
✓ Explore threats
✓ Link present actions to threats, past experiences and unwelcomed futures; delink inaccurate links

 Make Decisions

✓ Choose what will work best & is agreeable
✓ Specify who, what, when, where and how decisions will be implemented
✓ Settle on how outcomes will be recorded
✓ Set a future time to evaluate decisions

 Explore Possibilities

✓ Search for ways of interacting that allow differing cares to coexist without threat
✓ Expand thinking through questionstorming and brainstorming-do not censure or judge
✓ Reality test new possibilities

Figure 6: Phases of Insight Mediation

mediation as a process can be safe and fair, along with the opportunity to educate the parties if they decide to participate.

Mediation is a creative, flexible, and fluid process designed to reflect the nature of the parties and their specific needs. It also reflects the personality of the mediator, who is influenced by his or her training, world view, and preference for formality or informality. Mediation sessions are almost always held in private, neutral, and safe locations that are agreeable to the parties. The set-up might be boardroom style or more casual, occurring around a coffee table in comfortable chairs. When a large number of parties or groups is involved, the mediator might use a circle format as a creative and orderly way to determine who talks when, using a "talking feather" or other object to designate speaking times, or a format called the "Samoan Circle" where a small number of people talk together while others listen in. Mediation sessions can be set up to allow a party to bring along a friend or an advocate for support. A translator can be brought in if the parties have physical or mental challenges or do not speak the same language. Video conferencing can be used when parties live at opposite ends of the country or cannot be in the same room together. The fact that mediation is creative, flexible, and responsive to the nature of the parties makes it an attractive dispute-resolution option.

The insight mediator, as with other types of mediator, is not a decision maker – any outcomes reached through mediation are consensual and fashioned by the conflicting parties themselves. The insight mediator commits to being impartial and not to favour one party over another. But the mediator can never be totally "neutral." We all have preferences and unconscious biases that emerge from our cultural and social backgrounds that influence how and what we hear and thus what we understand. For this reason, the mediators, by his or her very presence, change the parties' interactions and, in turn, this changes the conflict dynamic.

While much of the practice illustrated in this chapter revolves around an interpersonal workplace dispute, insight mediation can be used in other contexts, especially those where there are strong relational dimensions, such as in families, organizations, communities, and churches. The process might look different than what is described here. Insight mediation is not a "one-size-fits-all" model; it is designed to be flexible, responsive, and creative. Let's look more closely at each of the five phases.

Phase 1: Attend to Process

In insight mediation the first joint session with the parties lasts for three or four hours; if the conflict is not resolved in that time, more sessions might be agreed upon. In some circumstances – such as family and divorce cases, long-standing disputes where there are years of interactions to discuss, or if a substantial amount of money or number of issues is involved – a series of sessions is more often the norm. In my practice, interpersonal disputes involving friends or co-workers are often completed in a three-to-four-hour period. This amount of time is usually sufficient for the parties to discuss their interpretations of threat and to gain new insights that alter defend patterns of interactions, allowing learning and change to occur. Anything less than three hours is usually insufficient, and anything more than half a day tends to be too tiring for everyone. That said, there are no hard-and-fast rules in mediation. The mediator and the parties together can decide on the length and format the mediation should take.

How the mediator begins the session is important. It provides cues to the parties about the mediator's style, confidence, and skill level, along with his or her overall willingness to listen and be non-judgmental. Listening with an open and curious mind is paramount in insight mediation. But this phase is not just about listening: the mediator is also responsible for ensuring that everyone understands how the mediation will be conducted and how the parties and the mediator will interact. It involves building rapport and ensuring that the parties understand that they control not only what is discussed, but what is agreed to. If done well, phase 1 lessens the anticipated threats of the parties as they begin to develop confidence in the mediator and in the process of mediation.

Each of the five phases in insight mediation has its own goal and complexity. Phase 1 is important because it sets the tone for the mediation. It demonstrates that the mediator will follow each party's conversation while simultaneously responding to their needs. This is the time for the mediator to demonstrate that he or she is fair, impartial, and non-judgmental, and can be a resource to the parties when the conversation becomes difficult. It is in this phase that confidence in the mediator and in the process must be built for the mediation to proceed successfully.

Phase 1 provides an opportunity for the mediator to convey that he or she can manage the process and provide a safe context for learning, while demonstrating recognition of each party's fundamental role in directing the content of the conversation. It is such an important phase that mediators-in-training will want to take the time to think about how they want to present themselves to the parties, then practise what they want to say so they can be clear, confident, and comfortable. No matter what style we choose to present, our role as mediator should demonstrate our ability to be curious, attentive, and responsive.

The concept of *responsive intentionality*, discussed in Chapters Two and Three, is central to how the insight mediator interacts with the parties. This means that the mediator follows the parties and does not lead them. Following involves listening closely to what the parties are saying and verifying to ensure understanding. In addition to conducting a process that is interactive, inclusive, and fair, in this first phase of mediation the mediator must also demonstrate the ability to listen and follow the parties' line of reasoning.

The insight mediator discusses roles and responsibilities in a way that is interactive and non-directive. By this I mean that the mediator aims to engage the parties in a discussion, rather than telling them how to act: "This is how I see my role here today. How do you see your role? What do you need from each other, and from me, and what can you do for each other to make this a safe learning dialogue?"

Insight mediators are taught to avoid following rigid scripts and to ensure their comments are appropriate to the circumstances and character of the parties in mediation. For instance, it would not make sense to ask disputing family members or friends if they have the authority to make their own decisions when they clearly do. Being genuine, caring, responsive, flexible, and creative is part of good mediation practice. Ensuring that opening comments are both personal and appropriate comes through the integration of theory into practice. Appendix A offers an example of an insight mediator's opening statement.

Demonstrating sincerity, caring, and competence takes time and practice. Less-experienced mediators would do well to reflect on the following questions as they work to strengthen their presence in this opening phase: Am I acting naturally, intuitively, genuinely, and creatively, or still following my checklist and doing what I think I am supposed to do? Does my talking respond to the parties' conversation or lead it? To what extent have I achieved some degree of unconscious competence in this first phase of mediation?

Phase 1 is when the parties need to understand about process, confidentiality, and protocols. It can be compared to musicians who learn songs using sheet music. As long as they rely only on the sheet music, their performance will be stiff and mechanical. Mediators, like musicians, do well if they can "get off the page" and "mediate from the heart." To do this, mediators need to practise their skills and to understand the theoretical base underlying the process.

Let's see how the mediator in our case study, "The Straw that Broke the Camel's Back," attends to the matter of process and rapport-building with the parties.

MEDIATOR: Hi, Micki. Hi, Les. I am glad you were able to make it today. I appreciate that it takes effort to come to mediation and face someone with whom you are in conflict. While mediation may not be easy, it is often successful in helping people deal with situations that they feel strongly about and find difficult. So, to begin today's session, and maybe settle us all down a bit, I am going to review some of what we talked about in pre-mediation. [Mediator demonstrates knowledge and ability to take some leadership.]

Let's begin with my role. As we discussed, my job is to help the two of you engage in a conversation where you'll come to better understand some of the decisions that you have made, what motivated those decisions, and how you feel about them, in a way that perhaps you have not understood before. To do that, I am going to listen very carefully for what it is that you are saying to each other. In particular, I will pay attention to your non-verbal exchanges and the way you are interacting, as these are often the cues that something is important to you. I will also help each of you listen to each other in a way that brings deeper understanding of what it is that each of you care about. In mediation we call this "listening to understand." What you will notice me doing from time to time is asking you what you each hear the other saying. This will ensure that your understanding of what is being said by each other is correct. This is important because conflict often escalates from mistaken interpretations, something we hope to try to correct here today.

I invite you to listen to each other with an open mind, paying particular attention to information that you may not have not heard before. Very often it is this new information, and its effect on you, that opens new pathways for resolving the situation.

I will notice your patterns of interaction, especially how you talk to each other. If I suspect that those ways of interacting may be blocking your ability to move forward, I will point them out so we can talk about it and see if there is another way of interacting that would be more fruitful for moving forward.

Do either of you have any questions about what I just said? Is there
anything you want to say before I go on? [Mediator invites participation.]
LES: No, I don't think so.
MEDIATOR [TO MICKI]: Does that sound okay?
Micki nods agreement.
MEDIATOR: Alright. So, to help us "listen to understand," I am going to ask
you to talk to each other openly, and be sure to share all that needs to
be said here today. I will also ask you to focus on what the situation has
been like for you, rather than blaming or accusing each other for what
has taken place. When we feel judged we want to defend ourselves, and
a defensive response is very often interpreted by the other as an attack
toward them. My job, in addition to listening, is to notice when those
interactions happen and try to change them. How does that sound?

After both parties nod agreement, the mediator continues.

Notice that, in the above dialogue, the mediator presents herself as
someone with knowledge about mediation and who is willing to take
responsibility for helping everyone get more comfortable in this early
part of the process. She knows from experience that it is normal for the
parties to be nervous coming to mediation, given the uncertainty of the
situation. She also knows that they are likely emotionally charged and
expecting to have to defend themselves, since this has been the predominant interaction throughout their conflict. The mediator is transparent about taking responsibility for establishing an environment
conducive to mediation, which gives the parties a sense of relief knowing that someone is there to help with their difficult situation. It is important to repeat that insight mediators are non-directive. In this phase,
as in others, they are clear, knowledgeable, and competent, helping the
parties to engage in dialogue and interactions that will help the session
be positive and productive.

Many of the points our case study mediator discusses are typical of
what is discussed at the beginning of most mediation sessions. For instance, in our example, the mediator talks about the process of mediation, the roles of the mediator and the parties, and some protocols for
ensuring a good discussion. Other points are also generally discussed
in this early phase, including:

- the process of mediation;
- the roles of the mediator and the parties;
- expectations of confidentiality from both the parties and the
mediator;

- helpful ways of interacting, such as listening to understand and using non-blaming, non-judgmental statements;
- the possibility of holding a private meeting or caucus;
- confirming if the parties have authority to make decisions on their own;
- checking to see if the parties are able to stay for the time agreed upon for the session; and
- determining who is responsible for any outcome documents and their form.

Expectations of confidentiality

It is extremely important to discuss confidentiality right at the outset of the mediation since it is critical that everyone be aware of what, if anything, needs to be shared with others outside the mediation. If there are limits to full confidentially, this needs to be known. For this reason, the mediator needs to ask each party about his or her expectations of confidentiality. The mediator also needs to state what, if any, limits to confidentiality he or she can offer the parties. If the parties cannot agree on the terms of confidentiality, a decision needs to be made about whether the mediation can even go ahead.

In our case study, confidentiality was important because one of the parties, Micki, was acting as the spokesperson for a group of her colleagues in the workplace. It was thus critical to know what information needed to be shared with them and if any decisions needed to be ratified by the group. Awareness of limits to confidentiality helps to establish the context of safety in the room and beyond. Expecting that everything said in mediation to be in confidence and later finding out it was shared with others can derail any progress made or agreements reached. Breaches of confidentiality can also place the parties in a worse situation than before they came to mediation, thus breaking the cardinal rule that "mediation should do no harm."

Let's look at how the mediator in our case study introduces the question of confidentiality.

MEDIATOR: Okay, let's start by talking about confidentiality. Please know that I have no reporting requirements to either management or staff. I do have to let the HR Director know that we have met and the mediation is concluded because he is the person who engaged me to mediate this situation. What that means is that I can, and will, keep your conversation today totally confidential and within the confines of these four walls. Is that clear?

Now, Micki, I know that you are representing your group, so I am wondering what decisions have been made between you and the group with respect to confidentiality. What are they expecting you will report back on, and what leeway have they given you in terms of making decisions with Les today? [Mediator opens with question about expectations.]

MICKI: Well, it was helpful in the pre-mediation to ask us to go away and think about that, and so our group has discussed confidentiality. We agreed that the conversation between Les and I is confidential, but that any decisions that come out of our discussions need to be shared with them. They also want me to share my impression of the tone of the conversation, as they are interested in any signals Les might be giving.

MEDIATOR: So, the details of what you and Les talk about today do not need to go back to the group, but any decisions do. Do decisions need to be ratified by them? [Mediator restates and confirms.]

MICKI: Yes, if there's anything to do with scheduling or anything else that involves them, then obviously I have to talk to them before making any decisions.

MEDIATOR: Right, so it will be important before we leave here today to be very clear about what information you need to take back to the group, as well as what decisions the group needs to ratify and how this will be done. [Mediator summarizes.]

MICKI [NODDING]: Yes.

MEDIATOR: Is there anything else you want to share about being the spokesperson for your group?

MICKI: I don't think so.

Having clarified with Micki, the spokesperson of the group, that the conversation between her and Les could be confidential but that all decisions would need to be ratified by the group, the mediator turns to Les and asks a similar question about decision making and confidentiality.

Notice that the mediator chooses not to explore Micki's comment about being asked by the group to report back on the "tone of the conversation," as clearly there was something behind that comment. This is an example of the mediator's using her knowledge and experience to choose between following the conversation or continuing with process. In this instance, the mediator chooses the latter because, first and foremost, it is still early in the mediation. Both parties need to be allowed to speak soon into the session to be reassured that the mediator is someone who will listen to both of them and provide them with voice legitimacy. Listening to the parties early in the process also shows the mediator's ability to provide the parties a fair and balanced session. Demonstrating impartiality by giving each party an opportunity to talk early on in the process is very important.

Deepening the understanding of what a party has said happens only after rapport and trust in the process have been built. Because it is so early in the mediation session, our case study mediator lets Micki know, when she summarizes each party's reporting requirements, that she has heard that the group also wants to be informed about tone of the discussions. When making process choices such as this, it is a good practice for the mediator to make note of it so that it is sure to be brought up later.

MEDIATOR: Okay, Les, let me ask you; what are your expectations in terms of confidentiality? Do you have to take information or decisions back to management? [Mediator confirms confidentiality.]

LES: Yes, well. Because management sent me here it shows their support for this mediation. They do want results, so they'll need to know what the results of this session are. Obviously they don't need to know the details. I am happy to keep the details of the conversation confidential, but whatever conclusions we arrive at will have to be communicated back to them.

MEDIATOR: And, do they have the final say about what can be agreed to here today, or do you have the authority to settle? [Mediator confirms authority to settle.]

LES: Obviously what they would like is for me to work something out that would avert more difficulty with the group. If I can work something out and present them with agreement that averts a protest, strike, or a complaint they would be very happy.

MEDIATOR: So, they are interested in hearing the results, not in making the decisions that lead to the results. Is that correct? [Mediator restates and confirms.]

LES: Exactly, they want results. If I tell them we did not get satisfactory results they will simply have to deal with the situation themselves and make a decision at that level.

MEDIATOR: In many ways you are both under similar reporting expectations. Micki, you need to take back to the group any decisions reached by you and Les. The group will need to ratify those decisions; you do not have authority to make decisions on your own. What you do have is permission from the group to keep the details of what was talked about confidential. The group would also like to know about the tone of these discussions.

And you, Les, need to inform management of any decisions that are made here today, but you have the final say. They are only looking for results, and have no expectation that you will share any of the details of today's conversation. [Mediator summarizes both parties' positions on confidentiality.]

Under those circumstances, are the two of you okay to proceed with having a conversation today? [Mediator confirms understanding and agreement to proceed.]

MICKI: Yes.

Les nods yes.

At this point the mediator has discussed the process the mediation will take, and has verified that the parties understand and are in agreement with that process, including issues of decision making, confidentiality, the role of the mediator, protocols, and the idea of listening to understand. She then goes on to see if there is there is agreement about time and that cell phones are turned off, and reviews process – in particular, listening and interacting.

MEDIATOR: Good. As we talked about in the pre-mediation, today will be a three-hour session. Should we need a little extra time to finish up, are you okay to stay for an extra half-hour or so?

Micki and Les indicate agreement.

MEDIATOR: Great. I may call a break at some point during those three hours, but if you need to break or need to use the facilities before that happens, feel free to let me know. I will also keep track of time and let you know when we are nearing our three-hour limit, so we have time to make decisions about next steps if it looks like we will not finish today.

Have you turned off your cell phones or other devices so we will not be interrupted?

Micki and Les nod yes.

MEDIATOR: Know that you have control over what is talked about today and that you are in charge of any outcomes that might be reached. I will lead the process in the beginning to get things started, but mostly it will be the two of you talking to each other while I listen and, from time to time, ensure understanding. This means that at times I will interject and paraphrase what you are saying to ensure what is being said is understood the way it was intended. I may also interrupt the process and suggest a different way of talking in order to shift your pattern of interaction if it does not appear that it is all that helpful in being able to really listen to each other.

This is your opportunity to have a conversation about the situation in the hope of resolving it in a way that you will both feel good about it. My job is to listen and ensure that you understand each other. And as I said, I will notice your patterns of interacting and, if necessary, suggest ways of talking differently. It is clear from the pre-mediation that you both feel strongly about this situation, and there is a lot at stake that is motivating you to resolve it to some level of satisfaction. Are there any questions or is there anything else that needs to be said before we start? [Pause.] Micki, are you ready to go?

MICKI: Yes, I am.

MEDIATOR: And Les, are you ready to begin?

LES: Yes, I am.

Helpful communication interactions

Increasingly I am struck by the inappropriateness of the mediator's laying down "ground rules" for how the parties should interact and talk. Establishing ground rules is directive and can appear patronizing, depicting parties as children needing discipline and control even before they interact with each other in mediation. A better approach is to ask the parties how they would like to be treated by each other in the mediation. This question is brought up in pre-mediation, and the parties are encouraged to think further about communication interactions and come prepared to talk about them in mediation. Raising issues of communication and interaction in the mediation session generally begins with asking each party what he or she needs to have a safe and productive conversation. For example: "What do you want to request of each other that would help you talk about the difficulties between you?" "What can you offer to do that will make the conversation go more smoothly and be more productive?" Questions such as these often elicit requests about being allowed to finish speaking without interruption, being treated with respect, being listened to, or offering to behave in this way. After this exchange the mediator might offer other suggestions that, based on experience, have helped to create an atmosphere for learning and change. The following exemplifies communication interactions to which the parties commonly agree.

MEDIATOR: As you have requested, and from my experience, mediation will work best if, when the other person is speaking, you listen for information that gives new meaning to the situation and helps you to better understand each other's perspective and actions. This involves waiting until each of you has finished talking before offering your point of view. Waiting your turn is likely to be hard at times given that your viewpoints clearly differ. My suggestion to prevent yourself from jumping in before it is your turn is that you jot your point down on the paper I provided. That way you can be sure to remember to raise it when it is your turn to speak.

Let me add that, when you do speak to each other, it is best to focus your comments on what this situation has been like for you, rather than attaching blame; it is very hard to listen when we feel judged. That is our goal today – to better understand what matters to each of you so you can find new ways of interacting that are less threatening and thus problematic.

Once again phase 1 provides the first opportunity for the mediator to build a relationship with the parties in joint session. For this reason it is important that he or she demonstrate confidence in the ability to help the parties talk about the things they could not talk about to each other on their own. The mediator knows that the parties are coming to the mediation uncertain, anxious, and even fearful, so their emotions are escalated. Being clear, confident, balanced, and focused can help to reduce the parties' anxieties by showing them, at the very beginning of the process, that they are in good hands.

To do phase 1 well takes practice. New mediators can practise opening statements on their own by recording, replaying, and assessing how natural and confident they sound. They can also practise with a friend or fellow learner in order to receive feedback. Many new mediators are fortunate enough to receive coaching in simulated mediation practice sessions.

Remember that each mediation is unique, so the mediator needs to be flexible and creative. Pre-mediation provides the mediator with information about the parties and the nature of the conflict to determine if, in phase 1, it makes sense to raise the possibility of a caucus, to inquire if the parties have authority to settle, or spend time discussing the format of an outcome document.

The possibility of a caucus

To caucus is to hold a private meeting with each of the parties individually during mediation. In insight mediation, caucusing is used very sparingly, if at all, and only when it is clear that the joint session is obstructing the ability of the parties to talk freely, or when continuing face-to-face discussions puts them in harm's way. Pre-mediation discussions often provide a "heads-up" that caucusing might be needed, and when this is the case it is discussed in the phase 1 of the mediation; otherwise it is generally not mentioned. The reason caucusing is seldom used in insight mediation is linked to the core theorem that mediation engages the parties in learning about self and other. It is when parties are in the same room listening to each other's stories that misinterpretations, incorrect assumptions, and mistaken meaning making are likely to be noticed and new insights produced.

In our case study with Les and Micki, the mediator does not raise the idea of caucusing because there is no reason to think that one might be needed. Had it become necessary to talk to the parties in private, she would have explained it at that point. If, in the pre-mediation, the parties had indicated that private meetings might be helpful or if the mediator had assessed that they might be needed because of high emotional levels, the number of parties, or the nature of the dispute, then caucusing would be mentioned. In long-standing disputes – for instance, in divorce mediation – where there have been lengthy and highly emotional interactions with pressure to be silent, or in intractable conflicts where speaking directly to a person might be too risky, caucusing likely would be necessary. Thus, the mediator needs to know how to use a caucus and to understand its limits. Some tips for how, when, and why to caucus can be found in Appendix B. For now it suffices to know that, if caucusing is expected, it is wise to have one or more rooms available so a party does not have to "hang around in the hallway" while a caucus with the other party is taking place.

An overarching question in relation to caucusing is, who am I caucusing for – me (as the mediator) or the parties? Less confident and less experienced mediators might resort to caucusing prematurely because they are uncomfortable with how the parties are talking, even though, for the parties, their way of talking is familiar and produces new information. On other occasions the mediator might think it is time to bring the mediation to a close, and uses a caucus to expedite agreement. Insight mediators are taught that the effective use of noticing, acknowledging, and reflecting emotion; listening to what matters; reducing threats-to-cares; being curious, rather than judgmental; and changing patterns of interaction can almost always keep the parties in the room talking and listening to each other.

Confirming time limits and the parties' decision making

It makes little sense for a mediator to ask the parties if they have authority to make their own decisions when it is obvious that they do – for instance, in mediations involving parents and children, spouses, or close friends. In less clear situations the answer to this question is likely to be discovered in pre-mediation. Even so, it is still useful in the first joint session to ask if there is anyone else who needs to be consulted before any agreement can be reached, to ensure that there are no surprises and so that the parties hear the answer from each other and show commitment to it.

The question about whether the parties can make their own decisions is especially important when the parties are representatives of a group and in business and legal matters where any agreement reached might need to be discussed outside the session before it is settled. Asking about authority to settle is common in workplace disputes involving harassment or human rights, where, for example, financial compensation or reinstatement is being considered and authority for these decisions lies with others. In our case study, authority to settle is an important question, so the mediator asks about Micki's directions from the group she is representing right at the beginning of the session. And she asks Les, the manager of the group, if he has authority to settle or if decisions need to be taken to a higher level.

Determining the format for verifying decisions

The format for how decisions are to be verified or recorded is also discussed in pre-mediation. This gives some guidance to the mediator about how necessary it will be to discuss this topic at the beginning of the mediation. Determining how decisions will be recorded or verified is influenced by the nature of the dispute and the parties. In some relationships shaking hands is as solid a commitment to honour decisions as writing them on paper and signing them. More formal outcome documents – sometimes referred to as "Memorandums of Understanding" (MOUs) – might be required by law; in those cases outcome decisions are written, either by the mediator or by a lawyer. If written by the mediator the common practice is to it have it reviewed by each party's lawyer or by a lawyer jointly agreed upon; in such cases it is prudent to discuss the writing of the MOU and ensure mutual understanding at the beginning of the mediation.

Since the writing of mediation decisions is frequently the responsibility of the mediator, he or she should have some knowledge of how to go about drafting an outcome document. A sample agreement is provided in Appendix D. For now, it is important to know that agreements should be reciprocal, balanced, and clear, as well as just and stable. When the mediator does assist the parties to put their decisions on paper, he or she is involved in recording in the parties' own words the decisions agreed to, as well as reviewing the decisions with the parties for accuracy and agreement. Agreeing to put in writing what the parties themselves have decided helps to ensure they will leave the mediation with mutual understanding.

Under no circumstances does the insight mediator decide what the parties should do. Furthermore, as with other practices, the insight mediator does not sign outcome documents – written agreements are a contract between the parties themselves. The mediator does not have the responsibility of enforcing an agreement, which might appear to be the case if his or her signature is included. Indeed, a mediator who is not a lawyer runs the risk of being accused of practising law illegally if he or she signs an outcome document.

Having clarified the process of mediation and received agreement from each party to continue with the mediation, the insight mediator transitions into phase 2, *broadening understanding*.

Phase 2: Broaden Understanding

Broadening understanding begins to surface each party's threat narrative. It commences with the mediator asking the parties to talk about how they hope their lives will improve as a result talking to each other. Asking about "hopes," rather than about problems, is a distinct feature of insight mediation. The hope question is meant to surface each party's "big picture" motive for coming to mediation. It deliberately avoids asking the parties what they want from the mediation by inviting them to share their vision for a better tomorrow. Here is how the mediator in our case study frames the hope question.

MEDIATOR: Okay. What I would like for you to do to get things started
is tell each other what you hope will be better for you, and for your
workplace, if you are able to talk about the things that concern you. In
other words, how do you hope talking to each other will improve things?
Which of you would like to begin?
[Pause of about seven seconds.]
LES: I can start.

The power of hope

Not asking about contentious issues or what the parties want from each
other typically minimizes the parties' need to defend themselves against
each other's versions of the problem or against their demands. It avoids
the "he said, she said" cycle of blaming others and defending oneself.
Both theory and experience show that the parties' opening statements
about the conflict situation almost always carry judgment and blame
directed at the other party. Feeling judged and blamed puts that party
in the position of feeling the need to defend his or her viewpoint and
experience.

As explained in Chapters Two and Three, asking about hopes, rather than issues, at the beginning of the mediation session is an attempt
to move the parties away from their current defend patterns of communication. If successful, it allows the parties to hear each other in
new ways, thus engaging them in the learning process very early in
the mediation.

Surfacing the parties' hopes for a better tomorrow is a relational question that produces new narratives, which begin to unsettle or disrupt a
party's certainty of knowing the other only as a threat. Bringing doubt
to the certainty of knowing all there is to know about others sparks a
natural curiosity to understand them and their actions. Through this
curiosity, learning can begin. Learning allows room for the parties to
wonder: "If you are not my enemy, then who are you?" "If you are not
trying to hurt me, then what are you trying to do?" "If I have this all
wrong, then what is right?" This openness to learning makes space for
incorrect information to be identified and for new understandings to be
formed; it makes room for the possibility of change. It is only through
the creation of some doubt in a party's conviction – some small space
for curiosity – that hearing something new and learning can occur. This
is a central tenet of insight mediation.

Individuals come to mediation prepared to defend the values they feel are threatened. This is not surprising, since, until then, feeling under attack has been their primary pattern of interaction. In some cases this pattern might have gone on for many years. Even though the parties are instructed in pre-mediation to think about how they hope changing the conflict through dialogue will make things better, the tendency is for a party to frame his or her hope as a demand. The insight mediator is trained to notice when a party states a demand, rather than a hope. Instead of paraphrasing the demand, the mediator attempts to get beneath the statement using layered questions designed to help the party name the value behind the demand. I explain both of these communication skills in Chapter Six.

Figures 7 and 8 graphically represent the defend cycle that perpetuates conflict and the cycle of change that occurs when a hope narrative is introduced into the discussion with the parties. The figures are intended to provide a simplistic overview of the processes; in actual fact, however, the processes are much more complicated.

Most mediators ask which party would like to speak first, which recognizes the principle of self-determination, a principle that guides not only insight mediation practice but other practices as well. If, however, there is a reason to invite one party to speak first – such as high anxiety or the power dynamics warranting that one person speak first in order for the session to be fair – then the mediator will provide an impartial rationale for choosing that individual. It is important to know that the party who tells his or her story first has an advantage because of the listener's tendency to defend against the speaker's version of the situation, rather than telling his or her own story. As a result, the second speaker's version of the conflict might never be told fully or might have a less significant part in the discussions. Being aware of this helps the mediator to notice if this is happening and to redirect the conversation in a way that ensures each party is telling his or her story and not just responding to the other party's story.

In this second phase, the mediator begins to *broaden* each party's threat story by using what was learned from the parties' responses about their hopes for a better tomorrow. Being able to surface a hope provides the mediator a place to broaden on information that is less likely to be interpreted by the party who is listening as an "attack." The mediator might say, "Talk a bit more about your vision of a better tomorrow." Or ask, "What needs to change for your hopes to be realized?" "What

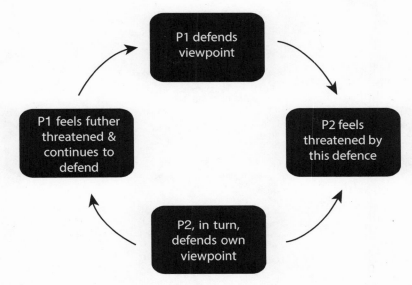

Figure 7: The Defend Cycle that Perpetuates Conflict (P = party)

has been blocking you from achieving your hopes on your own?" "What might be a way for us to begin talking that will get around those blockages?" When real hopes have been elicited, answers to questions such as these give the mediator data to explore that are less likely to produce defend reactions in the other party, thus leaving that party open to hearing new information and learning.

Let's listen in to the mediator in our case study to see how she works with broadening the threat-to-care story.

MEDIATOR: So, Les, what are you hoping will be better for you and your organization if you are able to talk to Micki about what you have come to talk to her about today?

LES: I would like to see some solution to the problem that's arisen, which is that the phones aren't being answered at lunchtime. And, the reason that the phones aren't being answered at lunchtime is because I went to bat for the folks to get the compressed hours even though my senior management wasn't crazy about the compressed hour arrangement. Now

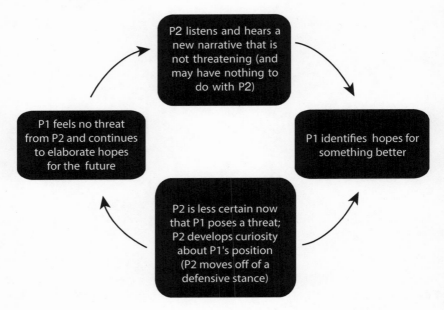

Figure 8: Identifying Hopes for the Future Provides Opportunities for New Learning by Reducing Threat

that we have compressed hours, which I went to bat to get for the folks and was able to get for them, we have this consequence of the phones not being answered at lunchtime. I had hoped that someone would come forward and give a hand in solving this problem. I was a bit astounded to find out that they weren't interested. If we can solve this problem and have the phones staffed at lunch, it seems to me that's cool, that's great. If we can't then we go back to the old arrangement.

MEDIATOR: You are really hopeful that if you can talk with Micki about the phones being answered or, at the moment, I guess not being answered, the situation of the compressed work week can be resolved and every-thing will be okay. [Mediator restates what she heard.]

LES: Yes.

MEDIATOR: Okay, and how are you hoping that would make things better for you? [Mediator asks an open-ended, exploring and curious question to elicit a hope.]

LES: That would solve the problem.

MEDIATOR: And solving the problem would make things good for you because ... [Mediator asks a layered question to clarify how things would be better.]

LES: The problem disappears.

MEDIATOR: Okay. We will have lots of time to talk more about how that would make the problem disappear, and what that means for you. We will also want to explore more about how the situation is impacting you now, and how solving the problem would affect you for the better.

Notice that the mediator does not continue to peruse what the problem's solution means for Les. She names it, acknowledges it, and clearly states that it will be explored later. Too much exploration of hopes this early in the conversation can be problematic, for two reasons. First, it can make the party feel that the mediator is in some way challenging what he or she is saying, thus increasing resistance even more. Second, balancing interactions at this early point in the mediation helps to build trust and demonstrate that the mediator is able to listen equally to both parties. In some ways, consideration of balance is similar to the point in phase 1 on page 65 when the mediator chooses not to probe Micki's comment about the group's wanting to know about the tone of the sessions. As we will see in the discussion of phase 3 and the section on deepening insights, balance is less of an issue when trust is built.

Let's continue.

MEDIATOR: So, Micki, let me ask you the same question. What do you want to talk about with Les here today, and what are you hoping will be better for you and the others if you are able to have that conversation?

MICKI: Well, I don't think the problem is going to disappear just with people answering the phones. I want to talk about the phones. I want to talk about the cancellation of the compressed work week in a really arbitrary way. And, I want to talk about lack of communication about how the telephone request was made, the lunchtime request, and how management treats us. This is part of a bigger picture about how management feels the admin staff can be treated. This problem isn't going to go away with a few people picking up the phone at lunch.

MEDIATOR: So, you want to talk about some of the same things as Les – the phones, answering the phones at lunch, the compressed work week. However, you see this situation as a bigger problem that has to do with management; it also has something to do with communication processes

at your workplace. If you are able to talk through these issues, what do
you hope will be changed for the better? [Mediator demonstrates the skill
of bridging, which involves paraphrasing what was heard followed by
an exploring question on the topic.]

MICKI: Well, I think if management starts treating the admin staff with more
respect, then I think that the admin staff can probably give more back;
that would make a better work place for people.

MEDIATOR: Making things better for everybody appears to be linked to
what you call respect. What respect means, and that the group does not
feel respected, is important for you to talk about today. [Mediator paraphrases and acknowledges.]

MICKI: Absolutely!

MEDIATOR: I would like each of you to tell me what you heard the other
say about their hopes for a better workplace. Micki, what did you hear
Les say he's hoping will be better after this mediation?

By asking this question, the mediator is trying to determine if, and how
well, the parties are able to hear each other. She particularly wants to
check if they have heard each other's hopes. More often than not it will
be discovered that parties' hopes are not so different, and this new information encourages the parties to continue.

Sometimes, however, it is not good to ask the parties to tell each other
what they heard each other say, especially early in the mediation. The
cue for knowing when and when not to ask a question of interpretation
comes through noticing how the parties are talking to each other. If they
are still quite judgmental and accusatory towards each other, then
openness to learning is likely blocked. Even if they did hear what was
said, they likely will be dismissive of the information. Less-experienced
mediators sometimes use this question as a crutch when they are unsure how to respond, and it can have unsuccessful results. Let's see
how well the parties in our case study are able to hear each other at this
early point in the mediation:

MICKI: That the problem would go away if we answer the phones.

MEDIATOR: It does seem he has linked the problem in that way. And, Les,
what are you hearing Micki say she is hoping will be better?

LES: Um, Okay. What I think Micki said was that she was hoping that the
admin people, senior management, should be treating the admin staff
with more respect. Senior management should be treating the admin staff
with more respect, that's what I heard you say.

MICKI [ADDING TO LES'S STATEMENT]: … as a core value of the company.

MEDIATOR: So, you were able to hear each other. This has good potential for being able to move forward and achieve your hopes. Where would you like to begin exploring? We can talk about the phones; we can talk about the compressed work week; we can talk about respect; we can talk about how you are being treated. Where would you like to begin?

The mediator, staying true to her earlier promise of letting the parties control what is to be discussed, invites the parties to choose from the issues that have been raised thus far. This question marks the transition to phase 3, *deepening insights* into why things matter and how they have become threatened.

Phase 2 is generally short. Its intent is to surface each party's hopes for a better tomorrow if the mediation discussions bring about positive change. The answers to this "hope" question provide the mediator an avenue of exploration that is less threatening and less offensive to the parties, thus altering the negative patterns of interaction that have given rise to and are sustaining the conflict.

Following the narratives that surface from the question of hopes for something better transitions the mediator into phase 3, where he or she begins to listen and deepen on information about each party's threats and how these are linked to the issues and interactions that are fuelling the conflict. Linking issues and actions to threats and cares is what will help the parties make sense of their interactions in a new light.

Phase 3: Deepen Insights

Phase 3 is the heart of insight mediation and it is where much of the "magic" occurs. In this phase the mediator helps the parties to explore and deepen the understanding of their threats-to-cares. Conceptually it queries the link that achieving what one party cares about must by necessity threaten what others care about. Learning about what is driving each other's involvement in the conflict presents the possibility that this link will be broken, thus allowing both sets of cares to coexist without threat. Working to break the certainty of this link is what insight mediators refer to as delinking, a skill I explain in Chapter Six.

Core statement of insight mediation practice

Deepening insights is a complex phase where the conceptual footings of the insight approach are evident in the mediator's responses and interventions, as reflected in the following core statement of practice:

Conflict emerges when individuals or groups experience threats to their desires and needs, expected patterns of cooperation, or deeply held judgments about social order that lead them respond defensively. Defend responses feel like threats to others and they too respond defensively thus creating defend patterns of interaction that sustain the conflict. Through deepening conversations a mediator assists parties to gain insights that produce new understandings and alter defend patterns of interaction so that learning and change can occur.

In phase 3 some of the more distinct skills and strategies used in insight mediation become evident, including deepening the understanding of threats, linking and delinking, finishing, and using. Showing how the mediator in our case study uses these skills might help to exemplify these micro skills in practice. In addition, there is a more complete explanation of them in Chapter Six.

Deepening insights involves discovering and exploring the threats that motivate the parties' actions. It also involves paying close attention to noticing and exploring what lies beneath the parties' feelings, since, as discussed in Chapter Three, feelings point to a value that is threatened. Feelings are linked to experiences from the past and to expectations of a dire future. When the parties discover how each other's present behaviour is linked to feelings from the past and projected into the future, they can begin to make sense of each other's actions, about which they were only able to make unfounded assumptions until then.

Shifting from knowing to curiosity

In phase 3 the mediator's role in facilitating learning is paramount. The mediator's efforts are focused on opening pathways for the parties to become curious about each other by expanding their data of experience and their understanding of those data. This often changes what the parties think they "know" about each other and about each other's intentions towards them.

When we think we know someone or something, we have little need to seek new information; our brain automatically follows the well-established pattern, the default position, of what we think we know. Our emotional investment in an issue also sends us back to our old patterns of thinking and interacting – even when we are wrong. We have no need to make sense of things in another way. Why would we? We already know. In this third phase the mediator focuses on helping the parties shift away from their knowing by encouraging them to question themselves and their actions as a way to develop new insight.

Curiosity is vital to generating insight. When we become curious we shift from defending what we know to asking questions about what we realize we do not know. In mediation, questions generated from genuine curiosity can lead to the discovery that each other's actions are rooted in values, and not simply motivated by ill will. This is an important discovery on the path to resolution: the parties can care about what others care about if those cares are not threatening what they value. This reconfiguring of meaning sets is what shifts the parties to work towards discovering a new form of interaction that is non-threatening, or at the very least less threatening. As we work our way through the dialogue from our case study, "The Straw that Broke the Camel's Back," I will point out the mediator's and the parties' interactions that illustrate these ideas to help them become clearer.

We re-enter the conversation at the point where the mediator asks Micki and Les which of the issues mentioned they would like to begin talking about. Notice that in this interaction Les is talking directly to Micki; however, the mediator responds to Les, rather than waiting for Micki to respond. This is intentional. The mediator knows from theory and experience that Micki is likely to respond in a defensive manner to Les's accusations, which for him will feel like an attack and either close down or serve to escalate his negatively framed comments. The mediator's strategy is to slow down the conversation in order to explore what Les wants Micki to know. The mediator does this by acknowledging his hurt feelings and deepening the understanding of them in a way that will be easier for Micki to hear.

LES: Let me jump in here. I feel this is a bit unfair right now. In a sense I feel we are on the same side. I work in the same climate of senior management that you folks do. They're a busy lot; it's a big organization. The wheels turn. Money doesn't grow on trees; it comes relatively hard earned in this business. I feel that within this climate I am asked to do a lot. I feel that I have tried to go to bat for you folks, for the admin staff. In this climate you can do some things and there's other things you can't do. When the consequences came out of this compressed work week that needed somebody to watch the phones at noon, I sort of figured, well ... I went to bat for you guys, let's see if we can deal with the consequences, so that we can live in this complicated, not entirely friendly world. I feel a bit betrayed.

MEDIATOR: And feeling betrayed is deeply troubling. [Mediator acknowledges the emotion.]

LES: Yes, it is.

MEDIATOR: And the feeling of being betrayed is linked to the idea that something is going on here that's not fair. [Mediator shows the skill of linking an expected pattern of interaction, which is a care involving Lonergan's second level of the good.]

LES: And so now I've got to fix the problem. Senior management is not going to fix the problem. They weren't even interested in the compressed work week solution in the first place. I had to fight for that, and now you are making my job impossible. All they see is productivity and results. Their solution is to go back to the way we had it. Frankly, I'm a bit tired, and I don't see any other way out.

MEDIATOR: Clearly, you were expecting something quite different from the staff than what happened. [Mediator restates content.]

LES: Yes, I was.

MEDIATOR: Which is partly why you are feeling so tired and confused by all of this. [Mediator reflects the party's emotion and links it to expectations.]

LES: Yes.

MEDIATOR: What were you expecting them to have done that they didn't do? [Mediator asks an exploring question about a care located at the second level of value: expected patterns of interaction.]

LES: I kind of thought that they'd see me as part of their team. And that, when a problem results from what I thought was a solution to the problem, they'd say "oh gee, well, yeah, let's fix this and make it work."

MEDIATOR: Had they done that, had they cooperated on the issue of the phones, what would they have been telling you? [Mediator asks a layered question about meaning making.]

LES: That they appreciated what I did for them. [Being appreciated surfaces as a care about being valued.]

MEDIATOR: And when that didn't happen, you were left feeling they were being so unfair and that they did not appreciate you. [Mediator names a threat-to-care that involves identity.]

LES: Yes.

As pointed out at the start of this excerpt of dialogue, the mediator responds to Les, rather than allowing Micki to respond to his view that he had been treated unfairly and was betrayed. This is important, and a good example of what an insight mediator is trained to do.

Noticing patterns of interaction

In insight mediation the mediator is highly attentive to noticing patterns of interaction between the parties that are judgmental, accusatory, and attach blame. The mediator knows that such responses are in defence of self. The mediator also knows that defend responses create in others the feeling of being attacked, and that these feelings trigger the need also to defend. This defend pattern of interaction blocks learning and interferes with efforts to change the conflict situation. Clearly, Les is defending. He thinks of himself as helping the group, he is on the group's side, his intentions are good, but he does not understand the group's response. He is confused; he wants to know.

The mediator hears Les's feelings of betrayal and confusion. From the theory of insight practice, she knows these feelings have led to an underlying care that, for Les, is threatened; his feelings point to a threat-to-care. The mediator also knows that this experience of threat motivates Les's actions, actions that Micki and her group take issue with because they threaten the cares that matter to them. The mediator will soon discover that the group's cares revolve around wanting to be valued and respected by the organization. When they felt disrespected, they took action by refusing to answer the phones over the lunch hour, time they felt they were "entitled" not to work. These threats-to-cares on both sides triggered the conflict.

From insight mediation theory, the mediator also knows that, had Micki responded to Les's accusation of betrayal, she would have felt the need to defend the group's actions, since betraying Les was not the group's intent. Once again, the mediator's theory of practice informed her that this would only escalate the conflict, since others interpret defend responses as an attack. What is needed is the opportunity to explore Les's threat-to-care.

Deepening the learning conversation

The above dialogue between Les and the mediator also exemplifies what insight mediators refer to as *deepening the conversation*, a key element of insight mediation.[1] Deepening engages parties in a learning conversation designed to surface the dynamics of their cares and threats. Deepening conversations help produce the learning moments and insights needed to shift the pattern of the parties' interactions from defence to a more cooperative relationship. It is a complex strategy that uses a variety of communication skills that characterize the insight

---

1 For an in-depth look at deepening conversations, see Picard and Jull (2011).

approach, including, but not limited to, noticing, listening to understand, exploring, asking layered questions, transparency, responsive intentionality, linking, delinking, verifying, sense making, finishing, and using. I describe each of these skills in Chapter Six.

Let's return to the dialogue and see where the mediator goes after she deepens the conversation on Les's feelings of betrayal and learns of his threat-to-care of not being appreciated when he had worked so hard to help the group obtain the compressed work week. The mediator turns to Micki.

MEDIATOR: Micki, what are you hearing Les say?

What might appear to be a simple question is another key strategy of insight mediation. The mediator knows, especially after deepening the conversation with Les, that it is time to invite Micki back into the conversation, and that it is critical she do this in a way that does not place Les back in a defensive stance. What Les needs most, after disclosing something as personal and potentially vulnerable as a care, is to be appreciated for his efforts to help the group and for being on its side, even though that is difficult. Most important, he needs to know that Micki has heard this. Thus, before exploring with Micki her cares and threats, the mediator intentionally checks to see if, and what, Micki has heard from the deepening conversation with Les. In addition to Les's knowing that Micki has heard him, it is also important for the mediator to know if Micki is ready to learn – that is, to accept new and likely contradictory knowledge. Let's see how Micki responds to this query from the mediator.

MICKI: Well, I hear you felt betrayed, and I'm sorry about that. But when you say that we are on the same side, that's where you are really wrong.

This response is typical of parties who still feel the need to defend themselves because something they value is at risk. This "sure, I get it, but" means that the mediator needs to notice the party's viewpoint and explore it, either then or later. Micki might well understand that Les feels betrayed, and she might be sincerely sorry for that, but it is unlikely in this instance that Les is able to hear what she understands or hear the apology she offers and that he so badly wants. Partly, this is because "but" as a conjunctive tends to negate the part of the message that comes before it. The other reason is that Les cannot help but feel defensive towards Micki's accusation that he is wrong. The mediator takes note of the apology and will come back to it when the parties are able to listen to each other and learn.

Having spent time deepening the conversation with Les, it is now important for the mediator to deepen it with Micki to ensure her views and threats are known. Picking up from Micki's last comment, the mediator explores what the group meant by saying "the two of them were not on the same side," as it contradicts Les's view that they are on the same side.

MEDIATOR: You don't see that that the two of you are on the same side? [Mediator clarifies.]

MICKI: We were on the same side until we got this obscure note asking if someone can staff the phones at lunch. When people didn't step up, then kapow! We learned then we were not on the same side. We saw that someone has more power who can use it by cancelling the compressed work week just like that (snaps her fingers) after six months of it working well. We saw more disrespect. We saw people being expected just to give up their lunch hour. So, you give us something and you take something away. We did appreciate it. We were on the same side. But then you took it away. You can pick sides, but we can't.

MEDIATOR: And so there was something in the note from Les, or in the way that the note was sent, asking you to cover the phones over the noon hour that left you feeling that you were no longer on the same side. [Mediator paraphrases to show understanding.]

It is often the seemingly small and unimportant interactions directly before a conflict comes out into the open that are key to understanding what the conflict is about. In the above excerpt, the mediator notices the request to cover the phones carried a strong negative message to the group. Noticing and naming it gives Micki an opportunity to explain the group's interpretation of the note and why it was important, thus helping to untangle some of the interactions that contributed to the problem.

MICKI: It was a kind of demanding note ... please sign up for lunch hour shifts, something like that. Well, we said, "no." We work hard, we've always had a lunch hour, and so people didn't sign up. Then the next day we get an e-mail saying "please be advised the compressed work week has been cancelled, Les." Come on, we deserve better than that!

MEDIATOR: So the actions that Les took left you feeling that you were not on the same side at all because he can make decisions and you can't. [Mediator makes another short paraphrase to let Micki know she is listening and to continue.]

MICKI: Yeah, yeah.

MEDIATOR: And so what did you interpret when that message came from Les to "please answer the phones"? [Mediator asks an exploring question about meaning making.]

MICKI: At lunch?

MEDIATOR: At lunch.

MICKI [WITH A GREAT DEAL OF EMOTION]: Well, we work hard. And yes, Les, you did work hard with senior management to get us our only speck of recognition in this consulting firm. But we haven't had a raise in ages. Where are all these cuts going to come from? Why do we keep being asked to do more with less? You yourself said the compressed work week is the least the company can do – right? – to acknowledge our efforts. So, fine, that is the least you can do. Now you are going to take away our lunch hours. So you give us something, then you take it back. There are some great things about this company, but they will take as much as they can get. This "please sign up for lunch hours" is so typical; here we go again, the other shoe has dropped. Right from the start, there were some people saying, "it's too good to be true." They wondered what would happen. Now we get this order to "sign up." So you give us the compressed work week, then take away our lunch hours. Some people think it was a set-up by management to take away the compressed work week for good!

MEDIATOR: What are you hearing Micki say, Les?

Notice the change in the mediator's intervention. Until now the mediator has been paraphrasing to ensure understanding about what each party has said. In this instance, she asks Les to do the paraphrasing instead. Why?

Having the parties restate what they have heard lets the mediator know if a party is able to listen and accept new information – in other words, it indicates their learning state. Recall that the mediator has just spent time with Les deepening the conversation on his cares. The mediator's theory of practice once again informs her that, when a person feels heard and understood, he or she is more likely to absorb and consider different viewpoints. Discovering if Les is able to restate what he heard Micki say – much of which was attacking and likely hard to hear – indicates if there has been a shift in his defences and thus a readiness to take in new data that could change his understanding of the situation and any subsequent actions.

> LES: Well I hear a lot of voices … different people. It's interesting to hear you say that everyone thought it was too good to be true, I will take that as sort of a backhanded compliment. You know I really did bust my ass to get that to happen for you folks.
>
> MICKI: We know.
>
> LES: And it was not easy; there are just so many hours in the day. I did that on my own time. Senior management did not want the compressed work week. And they still don't want it; they are the ones who want everything to go back to the original work week. I have to say that, when I look around this business and when I look around at the other firms, they are dropping like flies. They are folding, people are losing their jobs, times are tough. You know what it's like to run, or at least be in, this industry. There is a sense in which I am looking at my senior management and can't help but have a bit of sympathy for them. But, that having been said, you folks needed a break, and I figured that I would go to bat for you. There is no doubt that this problem we have now has to be solved. There's no doubt about it. If we start losing business, that means that eventually we'll start losing people. We are all in this together, so let's see if we can find a way out of it together. That's what I hope.

Notice in this dialogue another shift in Les's pattern of interaction. He is able to hear, to a degree at least, what Micki said. He has heard and accepted what he named as a compliment from the group. Then he returns to his defend story by further elaborating on his efforts to help the group. Towards the end of his dialogue, he offers a collaborative and shared hope that he and the group can work together for the benefit of everyone.

Also notice that the mediator stays clear of Les's defend story. Instead, she attempts to verify if Les really is able to hear the threats-to-cares from Micki and her group.

> MEDIATOR: So, when you were listening to what Micki was saying about what it felt like to be told that they had to answer the phones at lunch hour, what were you hearing Micki and the others saying that felt like?
>
> LES: Well, I have to say that what I heard her say was that she was being ordered peremptorily to work lunch hours with a veiled threat that the

other shoe will drop anyway. I don't think that's fair. I spent a bit of time trying to craft that e-mail, and I spent a bit of time trying actually to give a bit of information about the situation, but I wasn't ...

Although Les has heard Micki, he quickly dismisses the point and returns to defending himself. This elicits a defensive and attacking response from Micki.

MICKI [INTERRUPTING LES AND ACCUSING]: There was no craft to that e-mail, Les!

LES [DEFENDING]: But, I mean, look ...

At this point the mediator intervenes to change the defend pattern that is emerging by attempting to refocus the parties' attention on the data of experience that seemed to be generating new insights.

MEDIATOR: Let's keep the conversation going in the direction it was heading, because there seemed to be something important in your restating that the group experienced a veiled threat coming from you. My hunch is this: it is really hard for you to hear the team say that you were not going to bat for them, especially in the situation where you asked them to cover the phones over lunch.

LES: Yeah.

MEDIATOR: Yeah. So when you hear them say that was the last straw, and that losing their condensed work week was sort of expected, it's hard for you to hear that. [Mediator verifies the existence of a threat to Les's feelings.]

LES: Certainly it's hard for me to hear that. I tell you I feel caught in the middle. You know senior management, they are tough guys. I can go and whine about you folks or whatever. You know, they are not interested, they want the job done. They want the admin staff to be delivering the services so that they can bring in the money and sign the cheques for the money to go out. It's up to me to keep the wheels turning.

MICKI: Well, so what you are saying is what some of the staff also are saying. Management are tough – you don't have to tell us that. We know that the industry is tough, and we have heard this for a long time. It's been the justification for no pay raises, the justification for other cuts, and the justification for term employees, blah, blah, blah. We have heard this a lot.

LES: Right.

MICKI: You were able to stand up and get some things that we needed. But now people are saying that maybe you can't, maybe it's too much for you, and that's why there is a formal complaint, as you know, being discussed with head office. Because ultimately management also has to be accountable; you can't be the only one to be accountable for everything. They can't get blood out of a stone, that's what people are saying. So, in some ways, when we got the e-mail, it might have come from you, but a lot of people were thinking that it didn't come from you, that you were being told to take away the compressed work week. Sure, Les, we have had a good working relationship in the past. But sometimes it does get to be too much. It is not acceptable to treat people like that, and management has to hear that message. If they hear it this way, maybe they will finally get it!

LES: Can I say something in response to that? First of all, I appreciate a couple of things you said, Micki. I appreciate your sense that in some ways I am caught in this, and I am kind of on your side. I'll tell you what I think, though. I don't think this is a lot to ask, and I don't think that it's too much to say, "come on team, let's see if we can find a way of solving this problem." Once this problem goes away, then your compressed work week stays, and we keep the wolves at bay. We can keep a place here that's a bit sane.

Notice that the parties are talking more, and talking to each other. Also notice that the mediator is talking less. The parties' talking directly to each other is a significant shift that mediators need to notice and encourage. This shift from talking to the mediator to talking to each other reflects a job well done. But the mediator's job is not finished. He or she needs to continue to listen closely to determine if the exchanges between the parties are interpreted as explanations and elaborations, rather than as defend responses that need to be defended against. In our case study, the mediator knows this shift is occurring because the parties are taking in the new data of experience that are being offered and working with them. She also knows that there is still some uncertainty about each other's motives, so there will be times when responses are heard as attacks, generating defend responses. She continues to listen carefully in order to intervene when this happens.

MICKI: You don't think it's a lot to ask because you have pay raises, you get a lunch. So, of course, you don't think it's that much to ask. [Micki's rejection of Les's interpretation that it is not asking too much of the team to answer the phones triggers a defend response.]

LES: Is this what this is about? I get all the perks and you get nothing? [Les attempts to make sense of something that right now makes no sense.]

MICKI: It's not like this is what it's all about. But when you say it's not too much to ask …

MEDIATOR: For you, there is something about Les's request that is too much to ask. It is not just about answering the phone for you. It's a bigger piece of the picture that is connected to working for this company. [Mediator links an issue to a second-level value: the expected pattern of interaction.]

MICKI: And the way it was done, crafting that e-mail. I mean I get Les … well, anyway …

MEDIATOR: Let me separate a couple of things here. One of the things I was hearing very strongly from you, Micki, was it's not all about Les. In many ways the response had more to do with sending a message to management than to Les. [Mediator delinks the interpretation made by Les that the group's action was directed solely at him.]

MICKI: Yes.

MEDIATOR: And Les, you were saying that for you the group's actions felt like a real betrayal; you could only see their actions as directed at you. Because of that you experienced betrayal through what you thought was unfair treatment. You got the brunt of it.

It seems like it would be useful to separate the group's actions from their intent, to note what these actions were about, and whom they were directed towards. Doing so might clarify the meaning that was taken by you, Les, about what happened and why it is so different from the message Micki says the group was trying to send.

What I have been hearing Micki say is something to the effect of "we know you helped us, Les, and we appreciated it. But right now we can't take any more. It's not just about you, Les. You don't really have control. Something has to be done with management." [Mediator pauses for about three seconds for confirmation or denial by Micki.]

And in many ways, Les, you are not contradicting what the group is saying. You know that it is tough in the organization right now. In fact, you are experiencing much of the same treatment as the group. [Mediator pauses for confirmation from Les.]

What I am going to suggest is that you, Micki, talk a bit more about how the you and team felt about the way the message to answer the phones was delivered by Les. There seems to be something there that might help us make sense of the difference between your interpretation and Les's intent. What would you have expected that Les would have done differently? [Mediator seeks understanding about the group's expected pattern of interaction by Les if he were to show it respect.]

In this dialogue we see the mediator use a number of strategies to expand and deepen the parties' data of experience, including linking, delinking, and seeking understanding about expected patterns of interaction. This latter strategy reveals further touchy areas between the parties, as seen in the dialogue below.

MICKI: Well, two things. So, we get this "please sign up for the lunch hour shift."

MEDIATOR: And what was your interpretation of that message? [Mediator attempts to uncover meaning making and shift away from the defend story.]

MICKI: It wasn't a crafted letter; it was a one line e-mail ... [She is still defending.]

LES [INTERRUPTING]: Five lines. I had three lines on the top explaining the situation and then sign up for the shifts. [He hears her defending as an attack, causing him to defend.]

MICKI: Yeah, well. And there was something about senior management saying, I don't remember exactly, but something about services not being up to par, something about us not providing services. [Micki continues with her defend story.]

MEDIATOR: So, to you and the group, it was a directive. [Mediator verifies a previously stated interpretation.]

MICKI: Yes.

MEDIATOR: Given that you took it as a directive, it was very clear to you what to do. [Mediator links meaning making to action.]

But for you, Les, it was not framed that way. You actually put some thinking into it. [Mediator makes another attempt to delink interpretation and intent.]

LES: I'll tell you ... I don't know ... e-mails are not necessarily my best skill. I tried to make it an invitation. I tried to say, here's the situation, we are in this situation, here's an invitation where we can solve this together.

MICKI: Yeah.

MEDIATOR: So, Les, what are you hearing Micki say about why that message was missed? You intended to send that message as a genuine request; it didn't get heard. What message was heard instead from your e-mail? [Mediator is still attempting to delink interpretation from intent.]

LES: What did she hear me say?

MEDIATOR: Yes. What did the group interpret from your e-mail, not your intention?

LES: She says what she interpreted, what they interpreted, was a directive: "you've got to do this."

MEDIATOR: And that's hard for you to swallow because it was not intended as a directive. [Mediator delinks interpretation from intent.]

LES: No!

MEDIATOR: And, so what are they saying was wrong with their interpretation of it being a directive? [Mediator links meaning making and action.]

LES: Getting a directive?

MEDIATOR: From you, yes.

LES: Oh, yeah; I get that shit all the time. It's crap. I mean, you can't … I mean it hurts, you feel like your chain's being pulled all the time. [Les is identifying with the other party.]

MEDIATOR: So it's not hard for you to empathize with the team if that's what they took your e-mail to say.

LES: If that's the way they heard it, I get it! Welcome to my world [pauses for six seconds]. This is our world. I'm sorry if that's the way it came across. Why should I want to visit it on you when I hate it when it happens to me? But at the same time, it is what it is. You know that's the world that we work in. I am sorry. I can tell you that I didn't mean it.

[Pause of nine seconds; the silence allows this powerful statement of understanding by Les to resonate with Micki.]

Notice the shift that happens when Les gets the insight that the team experienced something from him that, although he never he intended, he can empathize with, since he receives similar treatment from his colleagues and he dislikes it a great deal. This recognition leads him to apologize and assure the team that he did not mean for them to feel as though he was giving them a directive. This shift is an important moment not to be missed by Micki. For this reason, the mediator checks in with the other party to ascertain if she has heard the apology and/or noticed the shift in the interaction.

MEDIATOR [TURNS TO MICKI AND ASKS IN A SOFT VOICE]: What are you hearing Les say? [Mediator checks for understanding.]

A further aspect worth noting at the end of this excerpt is the length of time between what Les says and when the mediator responds: close to ten seconds! In mediation this can feel like a very long time! Silence is important in mediation. Parties need time to take in new information, consider it, reflect on it, and make sense of it before responding to it. The mediator needs to ensure there is sufficient time for this to happen. Unfortunately, all too often mediators feel discomfort with silence and jump in prematurely to fill the space. Allowing silence is a powerful tool that takes confidence and skill to master.

Let's move now to a description of the fourth phase in insight mediation.

Phase 4: Explore Possibilities

Phase four transitions the parties from discussions that generate and verify new insights to surfacing and examining new ways of interacting that do not produce threats, thus changing the conflict between them. If resolution of all the issues is not possible, attention is given to helping the parties discover more satisfactory ways to live with their differences. In other words, this phase addresses the conceptual question: Knowing what is now known about ourselves and each other, what can we do together not to be in conflict any longer? This transition towards generating possibilities for change can be fairly seamless or the mediator might overtly suggest that it might be time to shift to discussing possibilities for change.

Exploring possibilities occurs after the parties have achieved new insight about each other and their patterns of interaction have shifted towards dialogue, rather than defence. When this is achieved, the mediator orients the parties towards discussing possibilities for change if the parties have not started to do this themselves. The conceptual question is: Given what you now know, what can you imagine doing that will improve relations between the two of you? This shift in the dialogue is intentional, transparent, and done with the permission of the parties. The mediator might say: I am wondering if it is time for each of you to begin to discuss some concrete ways to improve the situation. Or, given your new understanding of what happened to create this situation, are you ready to begin telling each other what might improve it and keep it from happening again?

After confirming that the parties are ready and able to begin the search for ways of interacting that improve things between them, the mediator asks open, elicitive questions that focus on the future: How do you want the staff to advise you of their concerns in the future? If you were to find yourselves in this situation again, how would you want to be approached? What have you learned today that will change how you act tomorrow? Would this way of acting be helpful to each of you? When you return to work tomorrow, what will you be looking for each other to do, or not to do, so that you do not have to wonder about each other's intentions?

In phase 4, the parties use their new understanding of each other to begin making a concrete plan of action designed to change for the better the problems between them. Feeling less threatened helps the parties feel less defensive and more open to the new possibilities that emerge through their learning conversations. But talking about new ways of interacting or negotiating the resolution of transactional issues is not always easy for the parties, since old patterns run deep and are hard to change. It is not surprising, then, that discussions aimed at change run the risk that threats will reappear. Because of this, the insight mediator is vigilant about noticing the patterns of interaction that are playing out. When the mediator notices that the parties' interactions are once again defensive, he or she intervenes and shares what is being noticed, and help the parties search for ways to change this emerging pattern.

In situations where new ways of interacting are not readily apparent and the parties are struggling to be concrete about future actions, the mediator might engage them in activities such as questionstorming, brainstorming, or, as some refer to it, "popcorning" ideas. The practice of brainstorming is familiar to most mediators, as it gets the parties using their creative energy and new understandings of each other to generate new possibilities for interaction, while withholding any evaluation or discussion until later. Questionstorming might be less familiar. In this practice, the parties are encouraged to take a step back and generate a list of questions that leads them closer to the right question that will give them the right answer. It focuses on getting clear all the questions that need to be raised and answered, and then converting them into actions. Although akin to brainstorming, questionstorming typically opens thinking, while answers might close down thinking. Whether brainstorming or questionstorming, the mediator generally records the ideas or questions on paper, flipchart, or white board. Then, after all the ideas and questions are generated, no matter how far-fetched, the mediator leads the parties through a discussion of each possibility separately to allow them to evaluate the strengths, weaknesses, and feasibility of each. This helps test assumptions and understanding, and provides a reality-check on feasibility.

Enabling self-determination

In phase 4, the insight mediator pays particular attention to self-determination – that is, the parties, not the mediator, determine the solutions. In fact the mediator refrains from offering any solutions. In this sense, insight mediation differs from some settlement-focused models where mediators tend to, and are often expected to, suggest options for resolution.

There might be times in insight mediation when the parties really are stuck for ideas. Then it is helpful if the mediator tentatively offers thoughts on moving forward; it is important, however, that the parties not feel any obligation to accept the mediator's suggestions. One way of framing suggestions might be to say something like: "I wonder if it might be worth looking at decisions others have reached in similar situations. I would be happy to share some of them with you if you thought it would help you to generate some of your own new ways of interacting. What do you think?"

There might also be situations when it is appropriate for the mediator to share with the parties his or her knowledge of statistical data or precedents that could affect their decision making. Once again, however – and it cannot be stressed strongly enough – the mediator should do this only as a last resort and in a way that is non-judgmental and tentative, rather than decisive or as a recommendation. More likely the mediator will suggest suspending the mediation to allow the parties to seek independent advice before finalizing any decisions.

Phase 4 focuses on helping the parties plan to do something different, which might require that they engage in give-and-take or accommodate each other's suggestions, so that they can reach an outcome that positively changes the pattern of interaction between them and resolves the issues in conflict. Some familiarity with negotiating strategies and conflict styles can help the mediator assist the parties in this phase.

Bringing closure to mediation before decisions are made

It is also important that the mediator know how to deal with situations where parties are not yet ready to make decisions. It is not uncommon that the time set for a mediation session is insufficient to discuss all the factors that are giving rise to the conflict and then to make a decision about each of them. When this happens, the mediator closes the session by focusing on where the parties want to go from that point. Sometimes the parties will choose to return to mediation to complete the process; at other times they will feel that the new communication patterns that have been established will allow them to continue the discussions on their own. In our case study mediation between Les and Micki, the session had to be closed before phase 3 was completed and before the parties were able to reach final decisions.

The dialogue that follows provides an example of closing the mediation before it is finished. It begins with the mediator recognizing the time constraints, acknowledging that there is more to talk about, and then summarizing what has been discussed thus far. This intervention allows the both mediator and the parties to focus their thoughts so they can determine what can be done in the time remaining.

It has been my experience that, when the parties realize they have little time left in the session, they often get down to the business of negotiating change. This is exactly what happened between Les and Micki. For this reason, it is best for the mediator to let the parties know that time is drawing to an end long enough in advance that some decision making can take place. I generally do this thirty to forty minutes before the agreed-upon time to close.

MEDIATOR: I see that we are just about to come to the end of our time here today. Clearly there is still more that needs to be talked about. What I'm thinking is that it would be a good time to recap what has been discussed, and then see where you each think you are and what you want to do in the time remaining.

After listening to both of you talk about the situation, I understand that you, Les, expected that your request for staff to cover the phones over the lunch hour would be a small thing to ask of them, as it would show their appreciation for the compressed work week. Yet, for you and the others in your group, Micki, covering the lunch hour was the last straw, as it showed a further lack of respect that people working in the organization have been experiencing. As a result, you each responded to the need to cover the phones over the lunch hour in very different ways.

For you and your group, Micki, the request deeply threatened what it means to work for this organization. And you, Les, experienced threats from the group and from management, leaving you wondering whether you are appreciated and whether you actually have any say in things. These different threats help to explain why you each reacted in the way you did. [Mediator summarizes the key points raised thus far.]

MICKI: Well, I'll tell you what, before we end I want to tell you that I am going to go and make a recommendation to my group that we do work the phones. Strategically I think it's going to be important to support you [Les] a little bit more. I am not sure that the other people are going to accept that. It all depends on how we are going to go forward with senior management.

From what you said there is a strong argument that you are going to need us. And because you are an ally for us, and I suspect from what you are hinting that, if you are in the centre of even more complaints, it may make you more vulnerable than we want you to be. So, I am telling you confidentially that's a recommendation I am going to make. We are going to need lots more discussion and openness from you, and we are also going to need you to set up some conversations with senior management. We need some dialogues, and you will need to sponsor them. If we give you this [covering the phones], we are going to need something in return.

LES: I can tell you that, in terms of the compressed work week, I can allow it to continue. We can keep it if we can solve the problem of answering the phones over the lunch hour. I can assure you that I can get senior management to keep it in place if I can fix their problem about the phones.

MICKI: In addition to the compressed work week, Les, there is also the bigger issue. We need some serious dialogues about respect in the workplace.

LES: There are some aspects related to that I can do; I will give it a shot. In terms of senior management, I can do my best to run interference and to go to bat for you, but there are some aspects in relation to them that I can't solve.

MICKI: Yeah. Les, what I am saying is that, if this recommendation I'm going to make to the team to pump you up by giving you what you want regarding the phones and to give you some credibility with senior management, and if we get the compressed work week back, we will also need you to tell management that we need to have some serious discussion about treatment of admin staff.

MEDIATOR: It sounds like managing the phone situation is a partial answer that does satisfy some of the things you need from each other. Discussions on how to improve the workplace are still needed. Les, you are saying that you can be part of facilitating a dialogue, you can help in some ways, but you cannot do it all. Clearly, change in the workplace is a whole other conversation that will take additional time to understand. [Mediator states progress and emphasizes that the larger issue of respect in the workplace still needs to be discussed.]

In this dialogue the mediator makes two important interventions. First, she reminds the parties of their progress and, second, she clearly names the issues that still need to be discussed.

Once again it is the parties who decide how the conversation will continue after the mediation. They can request a second session or they can decide to continue the discussion on their own. Feeling able to discuss unresolved issues without the aid of a mediator is fairly common at this point because interpretations of threat have been reduced and patterns of dialogue changed.

> MICKI: We need some kind of facilitated conversation that does not just involve you, Les.
>
> LES: Sure, we can do that. Once we get the immediate pressure of this situation off our backs, maybe we can brainstorm over a beer about it.
>
> MICKI: I don't think people are going to be willing to take off the immediate pressure. This is really serious, Les.
>
> MEDIATOR: Where would it be good to talk, if it's not over a beer? What would you imagine would be a way to begin the dialogue?
>
> MICKI: The beer or whatever is fine. It is when you talk about taking the pressure off that the problem arises. Changing the problem of the phones will not take the pressure off, Les.
>
> LES: Gotcha, gotcha, okay. I'm just talking about the pressure from this immediate phone problem. The pressure that I am feeling right now is that if we don't get the problem with the phones solved, then I am in deep doo-doo, and I won't have any way of solving it.
>
> MEDIATOR: Solving the phone problem takes some of the pressure off you, Les. [Mediator restates.]
>
> LES: So, if you are willing, as you said, to take that recommendation back to the folks, and if the folks are happy with that, then the immediate pressure is off my shoulders for now. That's the one I was talking about.
>
> MICKI: Then, if I'm going to do that, I have to go back with some pretty serious stuff about what they will get in exchange. If they are giving up their lunch, they will need some reassurance that this just is not another way of management cutting back.

In this excerpt of dialogue, we see the parties, freed of some of their threats, begin to negotiate decision making on their own accord. This is typical in my experience. The parties generally want to find ways to resolve their conflict – being in conflict is unpleasant! Removing threats might not resolve the conflict fully, but it usually opens a pathway for the parties to return to a more productive way of communicating as they begin the search to bring about positive change. In this example, Les is able to resolve the immediate problem of the phones in exchange for promising that he will do his best to ensure the group is given the opportunity to meet with senior management to discuss issues about treatment in the workplace.

Phase 5: Make Decisions

This fifth phase brings the mediation to a conclusion. It focuses on ensuring that the plan of action developed in phase 4 is fully understood and agreed to by the parties. It is the phase when the parties decide what they will do to make life better for themselves and for each other. Ideally the conflict will have been resolved, but in some instances resolution might mean finding ways to live with difference and disagreement – ways that produce more acceptable and less threatening ongoing interactions.

It is still a bit startling to me that, at this phase, when tensions have dissipated and planning for change is progressing well, it often happens that there is almost always something that has been misunderstood when agreements are being reviewed. Finding that out now helps to avoid problems in the future. It is the mediator's role to ensure that the parties clearly understand what they are agreeing to, and they do this by reviewing in great detail the who, what, where, and when of each solution proposed.

In insight mediation, as in many other mediation models, it is common for the parties' decisions to be put into writing, either in the form of a formal or legal document or in "lay" terminology. Written documents contain the details of each decision in separate and numbered paragraphs, and include some degree of reciprocity. Agreements are also balanced, meaning that the parties share the responsibility of taking action to make things better. They are deliberately free of jargon, and written in such a way that the parties can easily read and review them on their own if issues resurface. The parties discuss how reasonable, capable, and stable the terms are, as well as what they agree to do if the "plan of action" breaks down. The parties date and sign written agreements, and each party receives a copy. The mediator does not sign this document. A completed sample outcome document can be found in Appendix D.

Continuing with flexibility and creativity

Flexibility and creativity continue to be important in this final phase of the mediation. Outcome decisions belong to the parties, and therefore need to reflect the parties' wishes and needs. For example, the parties might be satisfied with simply shaking hands as a show of good faith for the decisions reached. Unless there are some legal reporting requirements, non-written agreements are acceptable and respected. The question of what method of recording outcome decisions the parties prefer or require is raised in pre-mediation. The formality and format of agreed-upon decisions are often dictated by the nature of the dispute and its setting. When lawyers are involved, they frequently take responsibility for drafting written agreements. Sometimes the parties themselves prefer to write agreements, then have them reviewed by their lawyer, the mediator, or a significant other before they are signed. In some contexts it is the mediator who writes out what each party promises to do.

In organizational or workplace situations, or when someone other than the parties is paying for the mediation, it is often the case that the mediator is required to report back in some form. What the mediator is to report is clearly stated and understood by everyone at the beginning of the mediation. The general practice is for the mediator to indicate in writing, over the phone, or in person that the mediation has been held and if it has resolved the dispute. The mediator rarely, if ever, shares details of the discussions or the decisions that have been made. Any limits to the mediator's ability to keep detailed information confidential are shared with the parties in pre-mediation, and the parties are reminded of these again at the start of the mediation session. The parties might also choose to allow more detailed reporting to referring agents. Thus, it is general practice that, before the close of the mediation, the mediator discusses the mechanics of any reporting that the parties need to do, reminding them about the confidentiality commitments they have made to each other.

The excerpt below depicts how the mediator closes the mediation session between Les and Micki.

MEDIATOR: So, Micki, there is lots there in what you just said, and we have not yet had a conversation about some of those points. In the interest of trying to close down today, I'm going to ask you: What are you imagining would need to happen to address those larger concerns, and how would you see that happening? You have mentioned a facilitated dialogue. What reassurance do you need now that you can take back to the team in order to tell them, here is where we are going, here's what we agreed to; it is not finished, and we have more talking to do? What do you need from Les or from anybody else to feel like you have something of importance to bring back to them?

MICKI: Well, what I've said is that I'm going to make the recommendation that we find a way to have the lunch hours covered. In exchange we need some kind of assurance from you, Les, that we are not going to get that kind of e-mail again. You have already told me that, and I believe you. I will pass it along, but we've seen that behaviour happen before.

LES: I can't instantly become a different animal overnight, but I'll give it a shot.

MICKI: We know you can do it because you've done it in the past. So, the second thing we need is some kind of agreement to have a facilitated dialogue. We need to be assured of some kind of longer conversation about admin staff in this consulting firm. And because it isn't only about you, we need some kind of dialogue that includes the management team. We do not want you to go back and say the problem is solved. Instead, you can say the phone problem is solved if we can have this dialogue. We will cover the phones over lunch hour on the condition that we have some kind of dialogue with management about admin staff working conditions.

LES: I'll tell you, one of my responsibilities as supervisor for you folks is working conditions. I am happy to go to bat for you as I have in the past, so you will be happier in the future. You do need to know that we work in a tough climate, it's not always going to be easy working here, but I'm happy to go to bat for you.

MICKI: Well, it's okay to say that. We are talking about working conditions and raises, and those are not your problem. We have bigger problems with management that we have to deal with. A dialogue session is one way to start, but we are also going to see what other kind of action we might need to take. In terms of the specific issue about the phones, while there are some conditions, I can assure you that I will make the recommendation to my group to work over the lunch hour.

MEDIATOR: Okay. Again, I am going to try to focus us so we can close the session today. What more, if anything, do each of you need to do to be able to take those recommendations that you have discussed regarding covering the phones over the lunch hour, and how, in the future, e-mails from you, Les, will be written differently, some assurance that ...

MICKI [INTERRUPTING THE MEDIATOR]: Talking.

MEDIATOR: Yes, you prefer that Les comes and talks to you, rather than sending e-mails. So, to continue, you would also like assurance about having a facilitated dialogue. Les, you have given some assurance about setting something like that up.

LES: I can set something up. I can see ...

MICKI [ONCE AGAIN INTERRUPTING]: And I gotta tell you, Les, that if that doesn't go through, you will see some very angry people, there's been some real ...

MEDIATOR: There is clearly still a lack of trust about these assurances by Les, Micki.

LES: I can do my job in respect to the compressed work week and setting up a dialogue. I cannot solve the bigger problems, but I can go to bat for you.

MICKI: Okay, I'm feeling a little more reassured by how confident you are right now, and that's really what I needed to hear from you.

MEDIATOR: Do you need anything more from him?

MICKI: No.

MEDIATOR [TURNING TO LES]: Do you need anything more from her?

LES: No ... thank you.

MEDIATOR: Well, you certainly did some hard work today and covered some of what was troublesome for each of you. You also made some decisions. It is a beginning; however, it is not the end. I will leave it with you, Les, to take it from here in terms of moving forward with a facilitated dialogue. Micki, you are going to go back to the team, make some recommendations, and see what happens from that.

If there is anything more either of you need from me, you both know how to reach me. Okay. Is there anything else needing to be said? Good work.

LES: Thank you.

MICKI: Thank you.

In this passage we see the mediator focusing the parties on what they need from each other now to be able to follow through on what they each have agreed to do. For Micki, this involves assurance that Les will take responsibility for arranging a dialogue with upper management and continue the compressed work week. In return, Micki assures Les that she will recommend to the team that the phones be covered over the lunch hour. In closing the mediation, the mediator clearly states those assurances and asks one more time if any further clarification or anything else is required.

How the mediator formally ends the mediation is both personal and flexible. Some mediators have rituals: shaking hands, special pens or places for signing agreements, celebratory salutes, or other culturally appropriate activities that recognize and congratulate the parties on their hard work and success.

To sum up this chapter on the process of insight mediation, the goal of an insight mediator is to help the parties gain insight into the threats that they, and others involved, are experiencing and the defend responses that lie beneath them. New insight disrupts the certainty of knowing each other only as a threat, making room for curiosity and dialogue focused on discovering new ways of interacting that resolve the situation or at least change it for the better.

Insight mediators, not unlike other mediators, are curious. They wonder, they listen, they explore, they deepen, they follow hunches, they acknowledge, they stay non-judgmental, and they are transparent. To this list of actions, they add linking, delinking, and verifying. They work to develop new perspectives and a more complete understanding of the conflict situation that incorporates the viewpoints of all involved. Every intervention is designed to generate new insights and to empower the parties to be self-determining. Mediators avoid problem-solving responses and replace them with a range of questions that evoke experiences, feelings, and hopes. Cultivating curiosity and opening pathways to learning about oneself and others leads the parties to find ways to address, and ideally to resolve, the patterns of interaction that have given rise to the conflict between them.

Chapter Five

Ensuring Appropriate Participation and Follow-up: Before and After Insight Mediation

This short chapter focuses on what happens before the mediation session takes place and what follows it. In insight mediation these two phases are called convening and follow-up. Nearly all mediators undertake pre- and post-mediation interventions, and there is considerable similarity in these practices; however, I also note those times when the mediator might do something less common.[1]

Convening can be done by the mediator or by an individual specifically designated for this function. It is common, for instance, in organizational, community, and volunteer mediation programs for the staff person with the most training experience to take on the convener role. In private practice, it is more likely that the convener and the mediator will be the same person. In the discussions that follow, the individual undertaking the work involved in the pre-mediation phase is considered the convener, regardless of whether or not that person is also the mediator.

Convening ensures that the parties are able to make a fully informed decision about participating in the process of mediation, and it allows the convener to make an informed decision about the parties' readiness and ability to participate. The convener needs to be certain that each party will be safe discussing the situation and that it will be fair for them to participate either on their own behalf or with the help of an advocate. The convener also has the opportunity as part of the pre-mediation phase to determine if the dispute itself is

---

1 An excellent discussion of convening and preparing for mediation can be found in Bishop et al. (2015, chap. 5).

negotiable and if the conflicting parties have the authority to change contentious issues.

Mediation is not a panacea. It is only one of many tools that can assist parties, groups, and communities in conflict. Processes such as litigation, arbitration, conciliation, fact finding, and private judging are examples of other available conflict-resolution options that might be more appropriate given the mediator's lack of authoritative decision-making power (see Bishop et al. 2015). Judges and arbitrators have the power to make decisions that are binding on the parties, and this might be what is needed.

The follow-up phase of mediation involves individual contact with each party in person or by telephone to see how things are going after mediation has been completed. If necessary, it allows the mediator to offer further assistance if the situation is not working out as planned. Follow-up is not about ensuring the enforcement of agreements. Outcome agreements are non-binding except in legal matters where a judge includes the mediation agreement in a judicial order, or in environmental and civil disputes that are ratified by a government agency or official. Even in these cases, the mediator is not responsible for enforcing mediation agreements and does not have the authority to do so.

Before the Joint Mediation Session

As noted, participation in mediation is not always the best dispute-resolution option. As a case in point, mediation would not be appropriate in situations of human rights or civil liberty violations, where one or more parties have made up their mind and are not open to learning, or when the matters in dispute are not open to being changed. These types of disputes are better addressed through processes that involve adjudicators, arbitrators, or decision makers. It is the job of the mediation convener to determine if conflicting parties belong in mediation and if they do participate that they will not be worse off for it. Pre-mediation is thus a critical phase of the process.

Mediation convening can take place in person, over the telephone, or online through e-mail, Skype, or other such video links.[2] Deciding which communication medium is appropriate depends upon various

---

2 For discussions of the many diverse and unique applications of doing conflict resolution online, see Abdel Wahab, Katsh, and Rainey (2012); and Katsh and Rifkin (2001).

circumstances: where the parties are located, how able they are to take time from work or other obligations to travel to the convener's office, how anxious or unsure they are about participating, the urgency of the decision making, and other such factors. The point is that the convener can be creative and flexible when determining the best way to communicate with the parties on a one-to-one basis. In insight mediation we prefer, if at all possible, to conduct face-to-face interviews when convening the mediation.

Individuals become involved in the pre-mediation phase through various channels. In some instances, they seek out the services of a mediator if they cannot resolve the dispute on their own. Self-referring often involves asking others if they know of a good mediator – word-of-mouth is still one of the best marketing tools in this field. If this is not successful, interested parties can search the Internet or Yellow Pages. They can also ask health care providers, social workers, clergy, or other professionals for the names of mediators they might interview. Disputing parties also might be referred by their employer or supervisor to an in-house mediation service or to a private practitioner, or be mandated by the courts to attend a pre-mediation information session. Some individuals arrive willing to use mediation; others might be uncertain and reluctant.

As with mediation itself, convening requires significant skills and knowledge. Conveners need good communication skills along with substantial knowledge about mediation and other dispute-resolution or regulatory processes that can deal with the conflict at hand. In insight mediation this phase can be carried out by the mediator or someone whose sole job is to convene mediations, as often happens in large organizations and institutions. Human resource professionals, union representatives, workplace supervisors, and community leaders also conduct initial assessments of conflicts to enable them to recommend mediation, but however the mediation comes about, a convener is still needed to assess and prepare the parties for mediation.

Convening serves three important functions: assessment, education, and planning. Assessment engages the convener and the parties in a process to determine whether or not participating in mediation would be appropriate, safe, and fair. The second function involves the convener in educating the parties about what will happen in the mediation, to ensure that they understand what the mediation session is and what it is not, and to be sure that the parties are making informed decisions about their participation. This educational role also helps prepare the parties to participate in mediation should the decision be made to go ahead. The third function involves planning for the mediation. Let's look at each of these functions in more depth.

Assessing the appropriateness of mediation

During the assessment stage, the convener collects information about the nature of both the dispute and the parties:

- What is the nature of the situation?
- How long has it been going on?
- What triggered it to come out in the open?
- Who else is involved?
- Is this situation open to being changed?
- How capable are the parties of participating in the process of mediation? What supports could help them participate more fully?
- How open are they to considering new options other than what they are now demanding?
- How are the parties communicating with each other?
- How different are parties' interactions now than in the past?
- How emotional are the parties, how are these emotions being expressed, and what are some of their emotional triggers?
- What have the parties done to try to resolve the situation?
- How might mediation make things better or worse?
- How are the power dynamics playing out between the parties?
- What, if any, special needs do the parties have?
- What cultural influences are affecting communication patterns, emotions, and behaviours?

Questions that maybe more tailored to the insight approach include:

- What has been the overall pattern of interaction, and how is it contributing to keeping the conflict going?
- How open is each party to the possibility of learning and achieving a new viewpoint?
- How threatening is the notion of changing his or her viewpoint, or to be found to be wrong?

Many of these questions are intended to help the convener to get the parties to reflect on their needs, motivations, and other choices for dealing with the situation, and to enable the parties to make an informed decision about their participation in mediation.

Educating the parties

Regardless of how the parties decide to use mediation, experience shows that few really understand what it is all about. So the convenor's second task is to educate the parties about the mediation process, which is a large part of preparing them for it. Discovering what the parties know about mediation and other dispute-resolution options available to them involves asking questions such as the following:

- Have you ever been involved in mediation before?
- Do you know of anyone who has participated in mediation? And if so, what have they told you about it?
- What are you expecting will happen if you participate in mediation? What do you not want to happen?
- Why do you think mediation will be helpful in this situation?
- What concerns you about going to mediation?
- What questions do you have that would help you to make a decision about participating in mediation?

The convener also focuses on discovering the nature of the parties as learners – for instance, are they patient or impatient, frightened or excited, open or closed to learning? – how certain each party is about the other, and if this certainty is blocking the parties' curiosity and capacity to learn. In short, the convener has the responsibility of educating the parties about the mediation process, the roles of the mediator and the parties, ways of interacting that are helpful in mediation, confidentiality, authority to settle, and how outcome decisions will be verified.

I cannot state too strongly that mediation is not a panacea. The convener plays a key role in ensuring that the parties understand what mediation is and is not, and that the parties are able to make an informed decision about their participation. To facilitate this education role, some conveners distribute brochures, pamphlets, videos, or other handouts so that the parties can review what was discussed in pre-mediation and have something concrete to share with others wanting to know more about what the party will be involved in doing.

Like other mediation practitioners, insight mediators often use a document known as a "Consent to Participate in Mediation," a form that is completed after the pre-mediation phase and then sent to the parties by e-mail or post to be reviewed before they attend the first joint session. This document specifies what the parties and the mediator are committing to do in mediation, thus providing an additional educational resource. It also contains logistical information about where and when the mediation will take place. The practice in insight mediation, as in many other models, is to review the document at the start of the first joint session and have each party and the mediator sign it as show of their commitment to the process of mediation it describes. A sample document can be found in Appendix C.

Planning the session and coaching the parties

In addition to meeting with the parties to develop an understanding of conflict resolution and decision making, the convener also helps them to develop interaction strategies and skills to prepare for mediation, which often places the convener in the role of "conflict coach." Making an informed plan about how best to carry out the mediation session requires that the convener collect information to answer these and other questions:

- Who is the best person to mediate this dispute?
- Where should it take place?
- How formal or informal should the setting be?
- Is it likely that caucusing will be used? If so, how many separate rooms are needed?
- Is accessibility an issue? How best can this be handled?
- What accommodations might be needed to help the parties participate in mediation (an advocate, a translator)?
- Who else needs to be there, and how should they be contacted?
- Will lawyers be present? If so, what role will they play?
- Do the parties have the authority to make their own decisions? If not, how will they contact decision makers in mediation?
- How do the parties want outcome decisions to be finalized (in writing, with a handshake, other)? If a written agreement is preferred, who will write it? Does it need ratification by others or by a lawyer?
- How soon can the first session be scheduled?
- What "homework" might help the parties prepare for the first session?

If the mediated plan is to be ratified by group members, boards of directors, senior executives, or other authorities, it is important to know this before the mediation begins. It is also important for the convener to be aware of any institutional policies, practices, or attitudes that might influence the decision-making process before the sessions begin to ensure that any decisions reached will be supported.

Often, in family mediation, one or both of the parties will be referred for counselling before they begin to mediate in joint sessions. In other instances, it might be decided that one or more parties could benefit from some individual coaching to help them feel ready to talk about what matters to them before attending the first session. It might even be agreed that a party or parties will have a coach with them during the sessions. Coaching the parties before they participate in mediation is becoming more and more common. In fact, in recent years, the field of conflict coaching has become very popular, with the publication of books on the subject[3] and the development of conflict-coaching qualification programs. Conflict coaching is a process of conflict intervention that involves a disputing party and a conflict specialist in face-to-face meetings with the goal of advancing the party's knowledge of conflict and his or her communication and conflict intervention skills. Providing individual conflict coaching to parties requires similar skills and knowledge to those of trained mediators.

Problem-solving-for-one (Tidwell 1997) is similar to conflict coaching in that it is designed for situations where only one party to a dispute is present for mediation. The process seeks to help the lone party develop conflict management plans and strategies. This form of dispute resolution is a growing area of specialization for individuals responsible for dealing with conflict in organizations and those working as executive coaches, human resources personnel, or in an ombudsman's office. As with mediation, the process of conflict coaching is flexible, yet structured; creative, yet embedded in theory. It is culturally sensitive, and seeks to attain the duel goals of party self-determination and empowerment.

Post-mediation and Follow-up

There is work for the mediator to do after the joint mediation sessions conclude. This phase of mediation, simply called follow-up, is not universal, but depends on the nature and context of the dispute and on the individual mediator's practice.

---

3 See, for instance, Jones and Brinkert (2008); and Noble (2012).

Follow-up involves activities such as preparing and sending the mediation report to the referring agent to ensure that it does not breach any confidentiality promises made in mediation. It can also involve drafting the outcome agreement, circulating it to the parties for review, and then having them return to sign it. The mediator might also have some involvement in monitoring the implementation of the agreement, steering it through the making of a consent order by the court, or in holding funds or documents until the agreement has been completed.

Insight mediators think it is important to touch base with the parties after mediation to see how they are doing even when no formal follow-up is required. Once again, individuality, flexibility, and creativity are essential ingredients in determining how best to approach the parties after mediation. Depending on the parties and their mediation encounter, it is natural to ask questions such as:

- How have you fared in implementing the decisions you agreed to in mediation?
- How are interactions and relations between the two of you now?
- Have relations improved?
- How are feeling about your experience in mediation?
- Upon reflection, was there anything I [the mediator] might have done differently to make it a better experience?
- Do you have any questions for me at this time?
- Would you use mediation again?

Conducting a more formal outcome evaluation of a mediation service or program also takes place in this phase. This activity is aimed at collecting information about the use of the service and its overall impact.

Becoming a Reflective Practitioner

After mediation it is always a good idea for mediators to take the time to reflect upon their experience, analyse their strengths and weaknesses, and evaluate how well their approach responded to the parties' needs and goals. This form of self-reflection is known as reflective practice, and it is strongly recommended in most mediation practices.[4]

---

4 For a discussion of reflective practice, see Lang and Taylor (2000); and Schon (1983).

Reflection-on-action can be done individually or with others. New mediators tend to use self-assessment tools that were part of their learning program, whereas more experienced mediators tend to develop a more individualized tool. The self-assessment tool used in the training of insight mediations at Carleton University is included in Appendix E. Some mediators are fortunate enough to have a mentor, while others belong to a community of practice groups that can be used as resources to discuss the events and emotions of a particular mediation. Co-mediators have the luxury of each other to analyse the effectiveness of their interventions. Whichever self-assessment tool is available, it is generally good practice to reflect immediately or soon after the mediation has concluded.

According to Lang and Taylor, "at the heart of reflective practice is the willingness to question, to explore, to delve into the unknown and the uncertain" (2000, 120). Because questions are the nucleus of reflective practice, the authors provide an inventory of questions to help mediators get into the habit of reflection (140). Here are a few post-session questions:

- How was this conflict similar to or different from other conflicts I have mediated?
- How useful was my theoretical approach in this conflict situation? Was I able to help the parties generate new insights and learn from each other?
- How did I respond to unexpected or novel events?
- Was I able to experiment with new interventions and what did I learn?
- How did the parties respond to my interventions and responses? Did they find them helpful? If not, in what ways could I have responded differently?
- How can I use the lessons from this experience?

Chapter Six

Facilitating the Dialogue:
Insight Mediation Skills and Strategies

In this chapter I describe generic mediation skills and the specialized communication skills and strategies the insight mediator uses. Other mediation practitioners are also likely to use these tools, since they need to have good listening practices and ways of asking questions that do not evoke in the parties in conflict feelings of being judged, because that would lead to defensiveness and resistance. Some skills are unique to the insight method, however, because of the insight mediator's attention to the parties' patterns of interaction and readiness to learn.

All insight mediation skills have a name. In part this is because those involved in advancing the insight approach have adopted a "practice-to-theory and theory-to-practice" research approach, which supports practice with theory while refining the theory based on practice. To do this, we need to be clear about what we are referring to. In addition, many of us are simultaneously engaged in teaching, mediating, and research, which requires vigilance to ensure that, when we talk to each other, we are talking about the same thing. Naming our actions has also helped transfer new ideas and skills more readily and accurately, and it has provided a way to observe and give feedback to each other and to our students. Although the names of these skills might be unfamiliar to other mediation practitioners, it would not be surprising if they were to discover that they use similar interventions but were not aware those skills had a name or were supported by theory.

Through the development and naming of communication skills and conflict interventions, it is hoped that all mediators and conflict specialists will become better practitioners.

Communication: The Pathway to Resolving Conflict

Communication, or the lack of it, plays a central role in creating, sustaining, and resolving conflict.[1] How a mediator understands the process of communication influences how he or she will facilitate the process of getting the parties talking to each other. Opening the doors of communication for the parties to resolve their differences on their own is the goal of mediation. It sounds simple, but achieving this goal is quite a complex task.

The insight mediator understands communication to be both interpretive and interactive (Sargent, Picard, and Jull 2011). It involves interpreting other people's messages, making meaning out of these interpretations, and then responding to them. The meanings individuals derive from the words or actions of others stem from internal cognitive schemas formed through acculturation, experiences, and feelings. Communication is socially and culturally rooted. Cognitive meaning sets or maps are unique to each of us. This is why similar actions, events, and words can be interpreted so differently. In mediation it is common to discover that misinterpretation generating from attribution bias[2] has contributed to, and sustains, the conflict. It is also often the case that this misinterpretation carries a more negative connotation than the sender of the message ever intended.[3]

Communication, like conflict, is a relational process. It involves the sending and receiving of messages through a speaker and a receiver. It is not, however, just about the coding and decoding of messages, as I talked about in my first book (Picard 2002). It involves more than trying to understand the intention behind the speaker's message. Its interpretive nature means that communication is as much about determining how the receiver understood the transmitted message as it is about understanding what the speaker intended to say. This is important, because our "reading" of another person influences how we act towards her or him.

More often, the insight mediator asks each party what he or she heard the other party say, rather than restate what the mediator heard the parties say. This shift in strategy helps the mediator to know if a

---

1 For other texts that talk about communication and conflict, see Bishop et al. (2015, chap. 4).

2 Recall from Chapter Two that attribution bias refers to the way in which we determine the cause of our own or others' behaviour.

3 For more on this phenomenon, see Canary and Spitzberg (1990); and Ross, Green, and House (1977).

person is able to listen, take in new information, and thus learn. When the parties are in strong defend patterns, the ability to listen to a different viewpoint is challenging, if not impossible. If the listener cannot hear what the speaker is saying, this alerts the mediator that the listener still feels under attack and is acting in a defend pattern of interaction. It says that more work is needed to help the parties feel less threatened if they are to become open to considering new information and be curious about each other.

In general, mediation trainers tend to emphasise the transmission of messages over the receiving of them. They speak very little about the role the receiver of a message plays in the generation of information that is independent of the speaker's wishes or intent. The tendency has been to speak as if all messages are intentional, and when messages are misinterpreted it is an attribution error on the part of the listener, requiring the mediator to help the speaker help the listener understand. Although this approach clearly has merit, understanding the process of learning helps the mediator realize that, if the listener is certain he or she knows all that is necessary to know about the other, he or she will block, consciously or unconsciously, what the speaker is saying. For this reason an intervention that does more than just clarify meaning needs to happen. I say more about this later.

Although it has been said before, it is worth repeating that mediators commonly experience that the meaning of the message one party sends is often perceived by the other party as different. This gap is not just one of misinterpretation; it is also based on culture, experience, meaning making, values, biases, and the certainty of thinking we already know all there is to know. It is also common to hear what we "expect" to hear, not what was said. Furthermore, our actions are often as much based on what we believe others think we should do as on doing what we think we should do. Each of these obstacles to good communication is a product of our environment and our socialization.

Why is it so hard to communicate what we want to say? Recall from Chapter Two that we each have unique cognitive maps to interpret what others are telling us, and that these maps can result in similar words, experiences, and actions having different meanings. In addition, we often anticipate what the speaker is going to say, and fill in the blanks rather than stay open to listening. We jump ahead in the conversation because we think at about 400 to 500 words per minute, but speak only at a rate of about 125 to 150 words (Picard 2002, 70). This leaves lots of time to anticipate and complete sentences for others or simply "tune out" because we are bored waiting for the person to finish speaking. As much as 75 per cent of oral communication is thought to be ignored, misunderstood, or quickly forgotten.

The reality is that we are always communicating; we are incapable of *not* communicating. Good communication practices are vital, not only in instances that involve conflict, but also in everyday interactions. Communication skills are life skills; lessening the divide between misinterpretation and intent can make everyday life more pleasurable.

With that overview of communication, let's move to a discussion of the skills and strategies for helping the parties learn more about themselves and others who bind them in the relational dynamic of conflict. I have organized these techniques into four broad sections, each of which is fluid and flexible as well as nonlinear and open to creative applications. They focus on: listening to understand, asking questions that broaden and deepen understanding, communication skills and strategies that are prominent in insight mediation, and communication skills and strategies commonly used by both insight and other mediators.

As you consider this examination of communication skills and strategies, it is important to bear in mind that writing about them, as I have, might make it appear that they are absolute in their application with no room for emergent creativity. This is not the case. In real life the mediator will want to use them with sincerity, flair, and imagination. They are "tools," and like any tool they require practice, confidence, and competence to be used well.

Listening to Understand

The majority of the work of the mediator involves listening, but it is more than just sitting across from someone nodding one's head from time to time and saying, "yes," "ah ha" or "go on." As a skill, listening takes time and practice to do well. Active listening, the listening skill that most mediators use, originated with Thomas Gordon, a widely recognized pioneer in teaching communication skills and conflict-resolution methods to parents, teachers, youth, organization managers, and employees.[4] Insight mediators refer to the skill of listening as "listening to understand" because of our focus on learning. Listening to understand serves the following purposes:

---

4 See, for instance, his books *Parent Effectiveness Training* (1970); *Teacher Effectiveness Training* (1974); and *Leader Effectiveness Training* (1977).

- verifying that what we understood the speaker to say is what he or she intended to say;
- demonstrating our interest in what someone is telling us;
- encouraging the speaker to say more;
- helping the speaker to reflect on what he or she has just said;
- checking our interpretation of non-verbal expressions; and
- supporting the expression of strong emotion.

Listening to understand involves mediators in all four of the operations of learning discussed in Chapter Three: experience, understanding, judgment, and decision. Here is how. First, mediators collect the data of experience through hearing and seeing. They listen with both their eyes and ears by paying attention to non-verbal and verbal messages. Second, using their unique cognitive maps, mediators process and make meaning from what they have heard. Third, they verify that their interpretation of what the speaker has said is consistent with the intended message. Fourth, after verifying understanding and valuing what they understand, mediators make decisions about what to do. This "doing" could involve, for instance, indicating that the speaker should continue, asking a question about what was said, inviting the other party to paraphrase what he or she heard, paraphrasing what the mediator heard, asking about new actions that would not produce threat, and so on.

Listening to understand does not elicit new information to explore, broaden, or deepen. The intent of restating content, reflecting emotion, or summarizing ideas and emotions is to ensure that what was heard was understood correctly, and to let the speaker know that the mediator is listening, has understood, and is following his or her storytelling. In this way the mediator is encouraging the speaker to continue to tell the stories in his or her own way. The mediator is intentionality responsive to, and acting in the service of, the party talking.

Mediators use various generic "tools" to help them follow a party's storytelling, including restating content and reflecting emotion, paraphrasing what was said, summarizing a number of key ideas or points, clarifying confusion, and validating the parties' efforts. Let's go more deeply into what each entails.

Restating content and reflecting emotion

All messages contain both content and emotion – facts and feelings (Picard 2002). Listeners need to be sure that they correctly understand both aspects of a speaker's message. Mediators use restating to confirm that we are correct in our interpretation of the facts, while reflecting verifies that we understand the emotion behind the facts. A restatement would sound like this: "You came to work on Monday and found the filing cabinet unlocked." A reflection would focus on the feeling: "When you saw this, you were worried that confidential documents might be missing."

For some mediators reflecting emotion can be difficult especially if their experience or culture tells them that it is not acceptable to express one's feelings openly. Expressing emotion well requires mediators to have a wide range of feeling words in their vocabulary. Here are some common expressions of feeling words that can help new or even experienced mediators broaden their repertoire for what the parties might be feeling; the list is far from complete, and you might want to expand upon it and create your own list of words:

abandoned	disappointed	idiotic
abused	displeased	ill-treated
accepted	disgruntled	impatient
afraid	disgusted	included
angry	dissatisfied	indifferent
annoyed	distressed	indignant
anxious	disturbed	irritated
appreciated	eager	insulted
apprehensive	ecstatic	interested
ashamed	embarrassed	irked
attacked	envious	jealous
blamed	excited	joyful
betrayed	excluded	let down
bored	exhausted	lonely
bothered	frightened	loved
cautious	frustrated	manipulated
cared for	glad	miserable
challenged	guilty	misunderstood
cold	happy	negative
comfortable	helpless	neglected
concerned	horrified	nervous
confident	hot	offended
curious	honoured	optimistic
deceived	humiliated	ostracized
depressed	hurt	outraged

pained	restless	thoughtful
perplexed	satisfied	trapped
powerful	scorned	troubled
powerless	sheepish	undecided
provoked	secure	undervalued
put down	shocked	uneasy
puzzled	sceptical	unhappy
rejected	slighted	uninterested
relieved	stressed	unnerved
sad	supported	unsure
resentful	surprised	upset
respected	suspicious	wonderful
responsible	sympathetic	worried

If the mediator does not name the feelings that have been expressed either verbally or non-verbally, it can inadvertently communicate to the sender that he or she needs to express the feeling more loudly because it was not heard, or it can run the risk of escalating strong feelings such as anger and frustration. Reflecting emotion is an important tool to de-escalate emotion – in fact, it is often thought of as one of the mediator's power tools, so it is well worth the effort to learn to use it well. Here are some examples: "You feel betrayed by her refusal to help with the extra work." "His interruptions leave you feeling disrespected." "You are worried that you will not pass the exam." "It makes you happy when you are told you have done a good job."

Although it is important to use this skill often, it is not necessary to restate content and reflect emotion every time an individual speaks – being "parrot-like" when listening to understand is likely to be viewed negatively. Theory and experience show that, if we miss the opportunity to restate a point because we did not hear it, or because we chose to ignore the emotion, thinking it might be too "hot," or because we simply missed the importance of the speaker's point, he or she will let us know. In some cases the speaker might simply tell us we missed the point and repeat it. In other instances, however, it could result in the speaker's becoming more emotionally charged or cause him or her to disengage from the conversation. Both of these responses say to the mediator: slow down here, there is something important that has been missed and needs to be explored. Noticing how the parties are responding to our intervention or how they are interacting with each other is a guide for what to say or do next. Listening to understand is key to acting with responsive intentionality, an important insight mediation concept that I discussed in Chapters Two and Three. Finally, it is important, when restating content and reflecting emotion, to remain impartial, not to agree or disagree with what was said, and to be very brief when paraphrasing what was said.

In the case of Les and Micki, there are many instances where the mediator restates and reflects. This first example occurs at the beginning of the mediation, in phase 2, after the mediator asks Les and Micki about their hopes for the mediation:

MEDIATOR: So, Les, what are you hoping will be better for you and your organization if you are able to talk to Micki about what you have come to talk to her about today? [Mediator asks the opening "hope" question.]

LES: I would like to see some solution to the problem that's arisen, which is that the phones aren't being answered at lunchtime. And, the reason that the phones aren't being answered at lunchtime is because I went to bat for the folks to get the compressed hours even though my senior management wasn't crazy about the compressed hour arrangement. Now that we have compressed hours, which I went to bat to get for the folks and was able to get for them, we have this situation of the phones not being answered at lunchtime. I had hoped that someone would come forward and give a hand in solving this problem. I was a bit astounded to find out that they weren't interested. If we can solve this problem and have the phones staffed at lunch, it seems to me that's cool, that's great. If we can't, then we go back to the old arrangement.

MEDIATOR: You are hopeful that, if you can talk with Micki about having the phones answered, the situation of the compressed work week can be resolved and everything will revert back to being okay. [Mediator restates briefly without agreement or judgment.]

LES: Yes.

Note the mediator's short and to-the-point restatement. Briefly restating a key idea encourages Les to continue talking because he knows the mediator is attentive. Being concise also ensures that the focus of the conversation is not on the mediator. By not agreeing or disagreeing, the mediator maintains impartiality. Here is another example of restating. Again, note the brevity of the mediator's response.

MEDIATOR: So, Micki, let me ask you the same question. What do you want to talk about with Les here today, and what are you hoping will be better for you and the others if you are able to have that conversation?

MICKI: Well, I don't think the problem is going to disappear just with people answering the phones. I want to talk about the phones. I want to talk about the cancellation of the compressed work week in a really arbitrary way. And I want to talk about the lack of communication about how the telephone request was made, the lunchtime request, and how management treats us. This is part of a bigger picture about how management feels the admin staff can be treated. This problem isn't going to go away with a few people picking up the phone at lunch.

MEDIATOR: So, you want to talk about some of the same things as Les – how the phones are answered at lunch and the compressed work week. You see this situation as a bigger problem, however, that has to do with management and communication processes at your workplace. [Mediator restates important points.]

In this excerpt the mediator reflects emotion:

LES: Let me jump in here. I feel this is a bit unfair right now. In a sense I feel we are on the same side. I work in the same climate of senior management that you folks do. They're a busy lot; it's a big organization. The wheels turn. Money doesn't grow on trees; it comes relatively hard earned in this business. I feel that within this climate I am asked to do a lot. I feel that I have tried to go to bat for you folks, for the admin staff. In this climate you can do some things and there's other things you can't do. When the consequences came out of this compressed work week that needed somebody to watch the phones at noon, I sort of figured, well ... I went to bat for you guys, let's see if we can deal with the consequences so that we can live in this complicated, not entirely friendly world. I feel a bit betrayed.

MEDIATOR: And feeling betrayed is deeply troubling. [Mediator reflects the emotion.]

LES: Yes, it is.

Again, note the succinctness and clarity with which the mediator reflects Les's emotion. Including too much of the content of the message would lessen the power of this skill. It is common for new mediators to be anxious about using the skill of restating and reflecting. They sometimes feel that they are being too formulaic, that they are stating the obvious or simply parroting the speaker. Listening to understand can sound that way if not done well. Here are three suggestions for lessening that possibility.

First, be genuine. The repetitive use of phrases, as well as including every detail, runs the risk of being seen as following prescribed steps, rather than being fully present, genuinely interested, and understanding what is being said.

Second, once you understand the concept of listening to understand, especially restating and reflecting, make it sound like you. Talk in a way that is natural while being true to the purpose of the skill. These same points apply to the skill of paraphrasing described below.

Third, be careful not to preface your response continually with statements such as: "What I hear you saying is …" "Do I understand you to say …?" "What I understand you to be telling me is …" Speaking in that way is neither natural nor authentic. Instead, say what it is you have understood, and include only the essence of the message, not all the details. For instance, instead of saying, "If I understand you correctly, you would like this to stop now," say "So, you would like this to stop now?"

The skill of paraphrasing

The skill of paraphrasing combines restating and reflecting as a way to verify our understanding, to check that we have heard both the facts and the feelings in the speaker's message. As with restating and reflecting, paraphrasing involves repeating succinctly in our own words the key ideas about the content and emotion of what was just said while withholding judgment. Verifying is a core skill in insight mediation linked to the third operation of learning. The best way to verify understanding is to capture the essence of what was said, rather than trying to recount every detail.

As with all of the listening skills mediators use, paraphrasing requires that we neither agree nor disagree – that we not sympathize or overidentify – with what was said by using statements such as: "I can see why you would be angry." "I know how you feel." "You are right to think that way." "I have been in that situation, too." The mediator needs to remain impartial about what the parties say, and to be careful not to favour one party's experience over another's unintentionally. Listening to understand takes into account both verbal and non-verbal messages about both facts and feelings. The mediator paraphrases emotion in this example: "Both of you have at different times expressed, 'I can't take any more; I am giving all I can give. Don't ask for anything more because it hurts.' For different reasons each of you is feeling exhausted and hurt."

Insight mediators are taught what to listen for and what, and what not, to paraphrase. Let me explain. Until the parties in conflict enter mediation, they have been exchanging defend stories through their defend interactions; recall from Chapter Two, page 28, the difference between defend and threat stories. Early in the mediation the parties are rarely able to listen for understanding, nor are they ready to learn about the other; they are in defend mode. It is not surprising, then, that, when given the first opportunity to speak in mediation, the parties begin by talking about why they are "right" and the other is "wrong." These are their defend stories. If the mediator paraphrases this information, it will keep the speaker talking in this way, which only serves to continue the defend pattern of interaction because the other party, upon hearing it, disagrees and prepares to rebut the points. Something different needs to take place if learning and change are to occur.

The something different that happens in insight mediation is that the mediator listens for the threats contained in the defend story. Rather than paraphrase the facts of the defend story, the mediator notices, paraphrases, then explores the parts of the defend story that contain the threats. Asking about a threat would sound something like this: "From what you have been telling us, you clearly anticipate something untold will come of this. What are you worried about?" "A lot has happened to confirm that if you do not act as you do, something bad will happen. What makes you so sure of this?"

Summarizing key points

Summarizing is another frequently used listening skill in mediation practice, in which the mediator lists what he or she heard about many points over time, rather than verifying one point at a time. Summarizing is often used to help refocus a conversation that seems to be going in circles. It can also be used when the mediator or the parties are uncertain about where to take the conversation next. Focusing on the key ideas that have been expressed thus far gives everyone a chance to reflect and think about the next steps. Summarizing is a useful tool to review progress, link important ideas, and establish a basis for moving forward.

The excerpt below shows the mediator in our case study summarizing key points about what each party has shared about their respective reporting expectations and the question of confidentiality. It begins with the mediator's restating what Les said about whether management needed to make the final decision on what is agreed to:

MEDIATOR: So, they want to hear about the results, more than make the decisions. [Mediator restates content to verify.]

LES: Exactly, they want results. If I tell them we did not get satisfactory results, they will simply have to deal with the situation themselves.

MEDIATOR: In many ways you are both under similar reporting expectations. Micki, you need to take back to the group any decisions reached by you and Les. The group will need to ratify those decisions; you do not have authority to make decisions on your own. What you do have is permission from the group to keep the details of what was talked about confidential. The group would also like to know about the tone of these discussions.

And you, Les, need to inform management of any decisions that are made here today, but you have the final say. They are only looking for results, and have no expectation that you will share any of the details of today's conversation. [Mediator summarizes both parties' views about who needs to be involved in decision making.]

Clarifying confusion and validating effort

Clarifying confusion is a communication tool we use when we are confused and do not understand what someone is telling us. Clarifying is *not* about seeking new information; we have other skills for that. Its purpose is to help us stay present and continue listening after verifying our understanding. When we are confused it is hard to keep listening to the speaker because we are trying to make sense of what the person is saying. Clarifying involves asking the speaker to repeat or explain what he or she just said. For example: "It would help if you would clarify that point for us." "What did you mean by that comment?" "I did not follow all that you said; perhaps you could repeat that last part for me."

Validating effort is used to acknowledge and show appreciation for the effort the party is making. Validating statements sound like this: "I can see that you find this difficult, and I appreciate your willingness to hang in for a bit longer." "I know you are working hard to avoid blaming him, and your efforts are not going unnoticed." "It is difficult to engage in conversations when you know you disagree so strongly. It has taken an effort to be here today, and you are both to be commended."

Responses and Interactions that Block Communication

Before concluding this section on listening to understand, it is useful to mention three responses that block learning conversations: 1) reassuring parties; 2) offering advice; and 3) diverting the conversation. These responses block learning because they substitute the mediator's knowing, valuing, and deciding for the party's. Below I explain the reason each of these responses is thought to block communication.

Reassuring the parties

Why is it a problem to reassure the parties in mediation? In day-to-day conversations, when we really know someone and they know us, reassuring is usually appreciated and helpful. In mediation, however, saying that "everything will be okay" runs the risk of minimizing a party's experience and stopping the conversation prematurely, because it reflects the mediator's narrative, not the party's. Often the mediator who attempts to smooth things over is being overly optimistic about a situation that he or she does not yet fully understand. Worse, it is a judgment that overlooks a party's feelings, and can suggest inadvertently that the party should not feel as he or she does. The intent behind reassuring might be well meaning, but the interpretation of that intent is often misjudged.

Offering advice

Offering advice to the parties in conflict, even when solicited, is problematic for a number of reasons. It can prevent a party from achieving a deeper understanding of what really matters and what is needed, because it closes off the conversation prematurely. In addition, if the advice is given before the problem has been fully explored and understood, it is likely to centre on the surface-level problem, not the deeper level where conflict resides. Furthermore, the advice a mediator gives is derived from his or her own experience, personality, values, and culture. What might be good advice for the mediator might not be good for the party. And offering advice can be misinterpreted to mean that you agree the party is unable to do his or her own problem solving, which can create dependence on the advice-giver and leave the speaker reluctant to continue disclosing personal or private information. Giving advice can inhibit the mediator's ability to help the parties uncover deeply rooted values and feelings that could help them both in the present and the future. Finally, giving advice assumes taking responsibility; if the advice does not work, it will be the mediator who is blamed, not the party.

Diverting the conversation

Diverting is a common communication response that we have all experienced and likely used. This response involves diverting attention from the speaker's problem onto something that relates to the listener. Although its intended use is to show empathy by recounting a similar experience that lets the speaker know he or she is not alone, the message that is often received is that the speaker's problem is less important than the listener's problem. A diverting response draws attention from one party to another, and can sound something like: "You think that is bad? Let me tell you about the situation that happened with my co-worker last week!" Or, "I know exactly what you mean. I had the same experience, and here is how I handled it." Diverting also has the effect of minimizing ideas and problems, sending the message that the speaker is unimportant, undervalued, or not respected.

It is problematic for the mediator to reassure a party that all will be well, to agree or disagree with what is being said, to offer advice, and to diagnose, even when such responses are meant to be helpful, empathetic, or comforting. The reason is that these responses involve the interpretation of another party's feelings and actions through the lens of the mediator's value system, not the party's. A party who feels judged tends to reject, resist, dismiss, or argue with the opinion of those who judge – in other words, the party defends.

Having discussed the key skills of listening for understanding, it is time to turn to the skills of asking questions that will broaden and deepen understanding. Again, many of these skills likely will be familiar to most mediators.

Asking Questions that Broaden and Deepen Understanding

Skills of exploration are critical to engaging in learning conversations. As with listening, at the core of exploring is being sincere and non-judgmental with our questions and statements in order to demonstrate an authentic, curious, open, and accepting mind. Being non-judgmental means we do not judge others based our own views and values of what might be a better way of acting, while being sincere means that we truly want to know something; we are not simply following prescribed steps.

Unfortunately, a party might experience our questions and comments as judgmental even when our intent is not to judge. When this happens, it is best to "notice" and then "explore" that interpretation, instead of rejecting it by trying to convince the person of our good intentions. Trying to convince someone they are wrong to feel or think as they do is a defending response, and serves only to keep them on the defensive.

Once we recognize that someone feels judged, it is best to shift from talking to listening, then explore what was interpreted through the use of a curious clarifying question. Here are a couple of examples of how to respond in a non-defensive way: "I see from your response that what I just said caused you to become defensive; what was it that you understood me to say?" "My comment was clearly not helpful; what did you think when I said that?"

Exploring questions are designed to enhance learning because they broaden and deepen what is known and elicit new insights. A cautionary note is warranted. Exploring questions might be difficult for the parties to answer because they tread on previously unexplored and sometimes private or risky territory. Yet, esteemed mediator Dr Kenneth Cloke, in his book, *Mediating Dangerously* (2001), encourages us to refrain from taking the easy route to compromise and settlement and not to be afraid to help the parties create choices for themselves by helping them explore their inner feelings and values.

What follows are some approaches to asking insightful and thought-provoking questions. As with listening, asking questions is a skill that takes considerable practice. Unfortunately, practice alone does not ensure that we will be correctly understood. For this reason, mediators must always be vigilant about noticing how others interpret our questions by observing how they respond to them. For instance, if our question opens the door to clarifying or providing new information, it was likely a good one; if, on the other hand, it results in defensive or closed reactions, then we can be assured that it was interpreted as judgmental or accusatory.

Basically the mediator uses two types of questions: closed questions and open questions.

Closed questions

Closed questions ask for a "yes" or "no" answer. Most often they are used to verify understanding or check in with the parties about something: "Are you okay to go on?" "Has she understood you?" "Have I got this right?" "Is there anything more you want to say?" Closed questions are useful at times during the mediation session, but they are used much less frequently than open questions. One reason for this is that there is a tendency for closed questions to be leading and directive – in other words, the answer to the question is embedded in them. For instance: "Have you thought about talking to her about it first?" "Will you be sending him an explanatory note?" "Did you ask for permission?" "Are you going to tell the team how badly he is feeling?"

Open questions

Open questions invite the parties to expand on what has already been said and what is known. They also encourage the speaker to provide new information and then go more deeply into that information. One way to know if you are asking an open question is to reflect on whether the question starts with what, when, where, who, how, and, to a lesser extent, why. Asking *why* has the tendency to make people feel as if they were wrong to do or say what they did, causing them to feel judged and to respond defensively, rather than openly. One way to change a *why* question is to ask a *what* question instead: "What made you think to do that?" A *why* question – "Why did you do that?" – produces a defence, while a *what* question tends to elicit an elaboration of understanding.

Open and closed questions are used for different purposes; as described below, they may broaden the conflict story or deepen it.

Broadening the story

A broadening question expands what is known by asking for more information. They are open questions that tend to ask about general and more ancillary data. Broadening aims to expand the story with questions such as: "What brought this situation on?" "Where did this take place?" "When did it happen?" "How long have you felt that way?" "What is your overall worry?" "What more can you say about your relationship?" Such questions help to build understanding of the specific situation or context as a foundation for deepening the learning conversation.

Deepening the story

Open questions can also be used to deepen the answers to broad questions. They explore the feelings, experience, or values that give meaning to what the parties are saying. Deepening aims to go beneath the facts with questions such as: "What is it about your day-to-day interactions that you find so difficult?" "Clearly, you expected she would do something different in that situation; what were you expecting that did not happen?" "As her mom, what do you see as your primary responsibility?"

In insight mediation, when a deepening question emerges from the answer to a question that was just asked, it is referred to as a "layered question." Layering is an important tool in the insight mediator's toolbox that I describe further below. For now it might help to think of a layered question in terms of the metaphor of peeling back the onion to discover what is at the core. The following is an example of layering as a communication strategy.

MEDIATOR: What is the nature of the interactions that are causing the difficulty between the two of you? [Mediator asks a broad question.]

EMPLOYEE: She is my supervisor and my "go-to" for help, but I rarely find her to be supportive or helpful.

MEDIATOR: "You feel unsupported when you approach your supervisor for help; talk about how you expect her as your "go to" person to respond to your requests for help." [Mediator listens to understand, then follows with a "bridging" question.]

EMPLOYEE: Well, for one thing, a supervisor does not criticize you and then hang you out to dry like she does. It leaves me feeling stupid and worries me.

MEDIATOR: You say you are worried; what are you imagining she is thinking about you that is so worrisome? [Mediator uses a bridging response.]

In addition to broadening or deepening the mediation dialogue, open questions can also be used to engage in fact finding, finding solutions to a problem, and discovering expected consequences.

Fact-finding questions

Fact-finding questions are used to surface concrete and specific information: "How much of what is talked about here today needs to be shared with the group?" "When can the two of you meet?" "How much time will that take you to gather the information and make your report?" "What amount of money are you thinking would be needed?" "What have you done to try and resolve this before today?" "When you tried that, what happened?"

Problem-solving questions

Questions that seek to find answers to problems are called problem-solving questions: "What is preventing you from trying something else now?" "What do you think is needed at this point?" "What would you suggest happen now given what you have learned today?" "How can you improve upon the suggestions that have been made?" "What can you do now?"

Open questions can be constructed in ways that empower the parties. Communication experts and trainers often use the term "appreciative inquiry"[5] to denote when questions focus on what is already right with a party or when the intent is to evoke stories that illuminate the party's strengths as discussed below.

Questions to discover the consequences

Consequential questions are just that – they ask about the consequences of actions. For instance: "What will be the impact of not reaching a joint decision to move forward today?" "If the group says no, then what will you do?" "If you run into problems with each other again, what would you likely do?" "If she is late again, what will happen?"

Empowering and appreciative questions

Empowering questions are generally directed at helping the parties draw upon previous experience, understandings, and decisions in search of possible actions that will help them to move forward: "Think back to a time when something similar happened – what did you do then that was helpful?" "What resources were you able to call upon then that might help now?" "What other strengths do you see yourself having that might be useful now?"

Appreciative questions are just that – they positively value the party or the situation. The aim of appreciative questioning is to draw out positive images for supporting change. They differ from the questions commonly used in the problem-solving approach because they are positively focused questions about what is right, best, or preferred,

---

5 See, for instance, Mohr and Watkins (2002); and Vogt, Brown, and Isaacs (2003).

rather than about what is wrong, as shown in these examples: "What's good about your relationship now that would be important not to lose?" "What opportunities are emerging from this dialogue?" "What's been your most important insight or discovery so far?" "If there was one thing that hasn't yet been said in order to reach a deeper level of understanding, what would that be?" "How can you support each other in taking the next steps?" "What unique contribution can each of you make?"

Before moving on to a discussion of strategies that are considered unique to the insight approach, here are two other strategies to elicit insight: 1) continuing or connecting thoughts; and 2) how silence can be as good as a question.

Connecting and carrying thoughts

Mediators use questions or statements that are short and to the point to connect and continue thoughts and to encourage the speaker to carry on with what he or she is saying. Some examples include: "Then what?" "What happened?" "How so?" "When was that?" "What now?" "Who is that?" "How's that?" "Say more." "Go on." "I'm listening." Another strategy is simply to use gestures such as hand movements, nodding the head, sitting forward in your chair, or facial expressions such as a raised eyebrow, a smile, or a frown that expresses curiosity and interest in continuing the learning dialogue.

Silence as a question

Silence can also act to elicit new information. It gives the speaker a chance to formulate his or her thoughts, to think more fully, and to puzzle over what is being discussed before speaking. Silence gives people time to reflect on what they have heard, and then to value and act on it. Too often the mediator tends to fill in silence because the silence is uncomfortable. Allowing silence to occur takes practice. Over time the mediator will develop confidence in knowing that a pause in the conversation is as effective as – and sometimes even more effective than – asking a question or making a comment. The mediator's confidence in silence is reinforced by the knowledge that, if the party breaks the silence first, that party has selected the direction to go in the learning conversation. If the mediator breaks the silence, there is a chance that the narrative will be redirected inadvertently and inappropriately.

Communication Skills and Strategies of Prominence in Insight Mediation

In this section, I examine a number of learning conversation skills and strategies that insight mediators use, including: deepening the conversation, exploring meaning making and interpretation, being transparent, bridging listening and exploring, finishing the conversation and using the information, linking thoughts and actions, delinking misunderstanding, and verifying insights. Although these skills are essential to the practice of insight mediation, it is likely that other mediation practitioners, intuitively or under a different name, use some of these skills because they are effective. What is different is that insight mediation training emphasizes their importance and teaches the learner to be intentional and proficient in their use. We begin with the strategy of *deepening the learning conversation,* which is at the apex of what distinguishes insight mediation from most other mediation models.

Deepening the learning conversation

Deepening the learning conversation is a complex skill that requires the integration of various communication skills and conflict-resolution strategies. By deepening the conversation, the insight mediator is able to help the parties understand why they feel threatened in their interactions with others and how these feelings of threat are creating the defend patterns of interaction that are sustaining or escalating the situation.

The decision to deepen the conversation begins with the skill of "noticing," mentioned in Chapter Three and elsewhere. Deepening is done with intent, and is in response to what the party has said or done. It exemplifies the mediator who is acting with responsive intention. Let's look more closely at when and how deepening happens.

The party's verbal and non-verbal messages imply that what he or she is saying carries strong importance. The mediator notices this, and wants to be sure that she and the other party correctly understand the intended message, so she verifies what she has noticed and heard by restating the content and reflecting the emotion of how she understands the message. For example: "When you talk about your daughter continually being out past curfew, I notice that you become quite agitated, perhaps even angry." To confirm this is an important issue, the mediator asks a closed question to verify her interpretation: "Am I right that this issue is at the core of your anger and that we need to spend time exploring what is so worrisome?" If the mother confirms her hunch, the mediator begins the process of deepening the conversation.

Because talking about things that really matter to us is often difficult, insight mediators generally begin the process of deepening by explaining to the parties where they intend to take the conversation. When they do this, they are using the skill of "transparency," which will be discussed shortly. Asking permission is also useful. For example: "Since you are telling us that this issue has strong importance, it makes sense to explore it more deeply. Are you OK if we do this now?" At times it might also be useful to alert one party that the mediator will be talking with the other party for an extended time, and to offer some suggestions as to how to make this exchange productive, as depicted in the following dialogue:

MEDIATOR: Lauren, I will be exploring this issue with your mom, and this may take some time, so while we are talking I am going to ask you to listen carefully for any information that is new or changes how you have been thinking about things. Once we are finished, I would like you to tell us what you heard your mom say. When I am sure that we both understand her, I will invite you to talk about what she said from your perspective, or you can talk about any other issue that is important to you. And, as with your mom, I will explore what you tell us to be sure we all understand what is important to you and why, and then ask your mom to summarize what she heard you say to make sure she does understand.

Note that the mediator does not ask the daughter for permission to deepen the conversation with her mother or vice versa. This would be inappropriate, because allowing one party to speak is not a decision that the other party makes.

Deepening the conversation begins by asking the mother an open, curious question: "What is it about Lauren's coming home late that is so upsetting for you?" The intent of this question is to begin to surface unwelcomed or dire consequences that the mother is imagining about her daughter when she is late, how it makes her feel, and why. After restating or reflecting the answer to the question, the mediator continues the conversation with a series of listening and exploring responses. Exploring interventions that combine listening to understand and a curious question that probes for insight – a skill insight mediators call "bridging" – sounds like this: "So, Claudette, Lauren's breaking her curfew is something that worries you. [Mediator restates content and reflects emotion.] What is it that is so worrisome?" [Mediator asks an open, threat-based question.] In this instance, the mediator chooses an open general question to broaden what is known, thereby allowing the mother to begin telling her narrative in her own way.

Curious questions that deepen understanding are referred to as "layered questions." Recall that a layered question emerges from the answer to the question before. The mediator continues this pattern of listening to understand, followed by asking layered questions until the party has fully elaborated what matters to him or her. When this happens, the mediator has "finished" deepening. The questions used to deepen the conversation are purposely open and non-judgmental; they come from wondering, and are intended to evoke curiosity in the listener. It is only when our curiosity is invoked that we begin to learn about ourselves in relation to those with whom we are in conflict. Understanding what is driving our conflict empowers us to discover ways of changing it.

Deepening the conversation is powerful because it helps to make sense of actions that previously made little sense, or implied intentional harm from others. Once the threat is removed or lessened, the parties become free to listen to each other because their need to defend themselves has also been reduced. Another way of saying this is that the learning process that constructed the experience of threat has been "disrupted," and a new process of learning has replaced it. With the help of the mediator, this new process of learning is one that holds the possibility of finding new ways of interacting that allow differing sets of cares to coexist.

Being transparent about intentions

It is always a good idea for the mediator to be transparent about his or her actions and intentions, no matter what theory of mediation is used. Helping the parties to help themselves is the mediator's job, and nothing the mediator does to realize this goal needs to be kept secret or hidden from the parties. Not being open and clear with the parties can interfere with the principle of self-determination, which is fundamental to many mediation approaches.

It has been my experience that the parties arrive at mediation with escalated emotions. They are uncertain about the process and a bit wary of it even after attending a pre-mediation educational meeting. Most have limited or no mediation experience, and what they do know tends to come from "horror" stories told by friends of friends who have participated in mediation. Moreover, until now, the parties' interactions with each other have been difficult. So it is not surprising that the parties worry that the mediator will judge them, find them at fault, cause them to lose face, or suggest they do something they would rather not do. The skill of transparency is setting the parties at ease by letting them know that there are no tricks or hidden agendas and that everything will be out in the open.

Transparency is a particularly useful skill for the mediator to employ when he or she is deepening the learning conversation, because the parties can find deepening for insight to be a bit frank, even challenging, especially if it happens before trust is built, leaving them feeling uncertain or wary. Before beginning a deepening conversation with a party, especially if it is the first time, it is a good idea to explain what you will be doing and why, and then ask permission to continue in this way.

The following two examples provide a sense of what being transparent might sound like when the mediator decides to deepen.

MEDIATOR: This last interaction tells me that it might be a good time to explore more deeply what you are hearing your mother say about coming home late and how it makes you feel. With your permission, I would like to delve more deeply into what it means to you to hear your mother saying those things, and why you react the way you do. My hope is that having this conversation may clarify some of your behaviour that is so confusing to your mom. Are you OK with that?

MEDIATOR: I am going to spend some time talking to each of you in more depth. While I am talking to one of you, I would ask that the other pay close attention and listen for new information that changes how you now view things. After I have finished talking with the first of you, I will ask the other to tell me what you heard before I invite you to talk more about what you think and feel. Are you OK to do this?

Being transparent as a mediator means you do not have a hidden agenda. Rather, you are open and honest with each party as you work with them to change the defensive nature of their interactions. Transparency can be very short and to the point: "I am uncertain about where to go now; do you have any ideas about what might be helpful at this point?" Or, "I am going to say something that might feel a bit confrontational, but please know that my intent is only to open up some new areas of discussion that might help us move forward."

Exploring meaning making and interpretation, especially threats

Meaning making and interpretation, as has been said many times, create conflict and are foundational to its resolution. Asking questions about interpretation is not unique to the insight mediation approach; it is, however, more central to that approach. The insight mediator engages conflicting parties in learning dialogues designed to generate new understanding and insight because, through insight, conflict can change.

In Chapters Two and Three, I discussed interpretive and interactionist viewpoints, the relational nature of human interaction and conflict, and the idea that, as human beings, we act not only to meet our self-interest and needs, but also in response to others. I bring this up again as a reminder of why insight mediators are so attentive to discover the sense making and interpretations of the parties. It is here that conflict emerges and builds, and it is here that it will be reduced or eliminated.

Asking about interpretation and meaning making sounds something like this: "What are you hearing me say?" "What do you hear her asking you?" "When that happened, what did you take from it?" "What does it mean to you when that happens?" "How are you making sense of the situation?" "What would make the most sense to you right now?" "Clearly, what she is saying is not what you thought; what did you think?"

Asking about interpretations of threat is more focused. Because these types of questions can be difficult to envision at first, here are some examples of threat-based questions:

What worries you about the suggestion?
What do imagine will happen if you do not put a stop to the situation?
What makes you so nervous about his actions?
What are the risks if your mom is not able to move in with you?
What are the dangers of letting her stay where she is?
What makes this situation so frightening and untenable?
Why is his suggestion such a worry for you?
What makes you think she doesn't value the efforts you have been
    making?
What makes you uneasy about that decision?
You seem worried by John's silence; what do you think he is thinking?
Not being thanked by John is upsetting; what does the lack of appreciation say to you?

What would you expect Nadia to have done if she did feel sorry about
the situation?
What is it that you are afraid of?
What would she have to do or say for you to trust that she will be OK?
Where's the worry in his request?
How could you move forward and not feel the need to protect
everyone?
Where is that certainty of threat coming from?
What would need to happen before you could begin to talk about that
request?
Where is your uncertainty coming from?
What would need to happen to lessen some of your worry?
You seem hesitant about that suggestion; what can you tell us about
your doubt that would help us understand it better?
His comment just triggered a negative response, what was that about?
There is something deeply troubling about all of this for you; what can
you tell us about your reaction?
What do you imagine will happen if you are not able to resolve this
conflict?
How will not solving it affect your relationship?
What do you believe will happen if Sam does not follow through with
your suggestion?
What are you hearing her say that makes you so defensive?
What are you hoping to prevent?

Finishing the learning conversation

"Finishing" the learning conversation means continuing to deepen on
what is being explored with a party until it appears there is nothing
further to discuss and there are no more questions to be asked. It means
that the mediator knowingly and intentionally completes the process
of probing for insight because it is clear the party feels satisfied that he
or she has been understood or now understands. When deepening is
finished, understanding has been both reached and verified, the party's threat-to-care is understood, and the reasons for his or her responses are known. Finishing generates the information needed to
help the parties' make collaborative decisions. Insight mediators are
trained to be attentive when the parties' threats-to-cares need exploring
and when their exploration has ended. Through the use of finishing,

the parties gain confidence in the mediator's ability to listen and probe without judgment.

Insight mediators are also taught that, having started a difficult and deepening conversation, it needs to be finished. Not finishing it will make that issue hard to return to later, because doing so can leave the speaker feeling dismissed or unimportant and thus reluctant to raise the issue later on. Starting to explore for understanding and insight and then not finishing the exploration can call into question the mediator's impartiality. This is especially likely to happen when the reason for not finishing is so the mediator can attend to the other party because he or she is concerned about balance. This is why, when deepening for insight, the experienced mediator knows it is less necessary to balance the interaction, and that trying to do so can send the very message the mediator is trying to prevent: partiality.

The mediator also knows that attending to the other party while deepening is often less necessary because the information being elicited is information the other party is interested in knowing, and for this reason he or she is likely listening carefully. The mediator can quickly verify this by noticing the party's non-verbal cues. If necessary, the party who is listening can be reassured that she or he will have the chance to say all that needs to be said about what matters once this conversation has concluded.

Finishing a deepening conversation often results in the discovery that what was once certain in the parties' minds becomes less certain, or "disrupted," thereby releasing the curiosity needed for new learning to take place.

As has been said numerous times, helping the parties to understand each other's threats, feelings, and responses frees them to wonder about ways of interacting that bring about change for the better.

Using the insights gained

The insight mediator "uses" the insights gained from a deepening conversation into threats and feelings in various ways. For instance, the mediator might name a threat-to-care or a feeling, then link it to an action taken by that party that is creating some of the conflict. For example: "So, when you daughter is late coming home, your first reaction is to worry that she has been in an accident. That worry turns to anger when she finally does come in and you know she is safe. Your response then is to ground her. The action of grounding is a way for you to protect her, and you. The problem of course, is that the grounding seems to have made things worse, not better." In this example the mediator acknowledges the mother's feeling, then links that feeling to her actions in relation to her daughter's breaking curfew. The mediator could also use the insights gained to link or delink experiences from the past with those of the present. For instance: "You told us earlier about your brother being in a bad car accident when he was a teenager, and that it took quite some time before anyone even realized this and help could be sent. Clearly, this event is linked to the strong fear that you have when your daughter is late."

Another way to use the skill of "using" is for the mediator, after verifying a new insight, to ask the party how that new knowledge might change things. For example: "Given what you now know about how your fears are so tied into your brother's accident, what kinds of things could your daughter do when she knows she is going to be late to make the situation better for you?" The process of using ensures that what is learned through the mediator's interventions, especially after deepening, is used in the search for more acceptable ways for conflicting parties to interact.

The importance of verifying

As I said before, insights can be wrong! For this reason a mediator must be vigilant about ensuring that what he or she heard accurately reflects what was said; this skill is called "verifying." Statements such as "Oh, I get it now," or "I see what you mean," "I know," or "I understand" are always followed up with a question that seeks to discover what it is that the speaker now knows or understands: "You say you understand why your mother is angry at you for coming home late, it would be good to hear what you heard her anger is all about in your own words." Verifying can be as simple as checking out what you heard: "Am I right in hearing you say that this behaviour has to stop before you can begin to trust her with anything?" Recall that verifying if our understanding is correct occurs at the third operation of learning.

The skill of bridging

Bridging was briefly mentioned in the previous discussion about deepening the conversation, but it is worth mentioning again because it is such a frequently used skill. And although bridging might appear simplistic, it can be a powerful tool to move the dialogue forward because it demonstrates that the mediator is both listening intently and interested.

Bridging is a connecting strategy where the mediator first lets the speaker know he or she is listening by restating the content or reflecting the emotion of the speaker's message, then immediately following this with a curious question designed to learn more about the care, threat, intent, interpretation, or assumption behind the speaker's message. A bridging statement sounds like this: "You are clearly upset by what you consider to be a blatant refusal by your daughter to take this issue seriously." [Mediator paraphrases content and emotion.] "What would your daughter have to do to show you that she is taking the issue seriously?" [Mediator asks an open question looking for information on an expected pattern of interaction.]

Using the skill of bridging while deepening the learning conversation is essential. Asking a series of questions without "listening" first more often than not comes across as an "interrogation," "grilling," or "drilling down," rather than an exploratory curious conversation intended to help the parties. If experienced in this way, it would close down the conversation, rather than open it up. Bridging shows the mediator is listening, sensitive, and interested in learning more. Here is another example: "When your mom interrupts, what you are trying to tell her?" [Mediator restates content.] "What is it that you hear her telling you?" [Mediator asks an open question seeking meaning making.]

Linking the present to the past and future; delinking incorrect links

Linking is a strategy that involves listening for and asking about how threats-to-cares are connected to current actions and demands. It also tries to connect current actions and demands with past experiences and unwelcome or dire expectations of the future. The learning approach informs the mediator that the actions of the conflicting parties are likely linked to past experiences or feelings that they are trying to prevent in the future.

Linking involves finding out what the parties' feelings and experiences are about – in other words, what values and feelings connected to these values are driving the conflict. Linking produces direct insight into the values that the parties sometimes are unaware they are even defending. Linking makes sense of how these values are influencing the parties' actions and how they have contributed to the conflict situation. Figure 9 shows this relationship of the present to the past and future.

Remembered Past	↔	Present	↔	Anticipated Future
Events		Actions		Negative Outcomes
Emotions		Feelings		Imagined unwelcome or dire future
Beliefs		Actions		An event to be avoided at all cost
Background		Attitudes		
Values		Defend Responses		
Culture		Reactions		

Figure 9: Linking Present Experiences to Those of the Past and Future

Seeking to understand how one party's cares are linked to what threatens the other party is the goal of linking. Linking might involve asking a direct question such as: "So, how is your daughter's coming in late linked to your brother's accident so many years ago?" Or the mediator might simply state the link that seems to exist: "It seems that your reaction to your daughter's coming in late is somehow linked to your brother's accident."

The skill of linking requires the mediator to discover how past history is linked to current feelings. The intent is to explore whether something similar to what is happening now might have happened in the past, and if it did, how that is affecting the party's current attitude or behaviour. The mediator also asks consequential questions, then listens closely for how the party's attitude and position are linked to how he or she imagines the future. A consequential question would sound like this: "So, what are you imagining has happened to your daughter when she is late?" Or, "What is it that you're trying to protect your daughter from?" Surfacing the links that the parties are making to the past and the future helps them gain insight into the reality of those links in the present.

When a link is discovered to be not necessarily so, the mediator's attention becomes directed towards inquiring about the possibilities for new interpretations, using the skill of "delinking." Delinking occurs when the information and assumptions the parties are using to form the links they are making between events are discovered to be incorrect or incomplete and when the line of inquiry the parties have been following is replaced by a more useful one. Delinking distinguishes past experiences and imagined futures from present feelings. It helps to contextualize these three time frames by helping the parties knowingly link a past experience with a present feeling, or a present feeling with an imagined outcome. Doing this creates the potential for insights such as: "If my past experience of my brother's accident is driving these strong feelings of fear, then perhaps my daughter's being late is not such a threat after all." Or, "If this fear is linked to my brother, perhaps my daughter and I can find a way to lessen my fear when she is late." Or, "Maybe my imagination about what will happen to her is wrong." These new understandings lead to new decisions for interacting.

Delinking disrupts what is currently known, which opens up space for new learning to occur. Through delinking, interpersonal connections become more apparent, and others involved in the conflict become more than just "objects" of that conflict. Reducing or removing the threats to one party that have been linked to what matters to the other party, and vice versa, provides the opportunity for the parties to search for collaborative solutions to their shared problem.

Communication Skills Most Mediators Use

Opening the doors of blocked communication in the search for collaborative decision making is a task that insight mediators share with other mediators. Given this shared goal, it is not surprising that some of the communication skills insight mediators use are also used by mediators trained in other models. These overlapping skills include immediacy, confronting discrepancy, normalizing, "temperature taking" and asking for feedback, and verbal support. Let's look at these skills.

Immediacy

Immediacy is a communication skill that attends to what is happening "in the moment." It allows strong reactions or emotions to be dealt with as they emerge. Working in the "here and now" helps to keep the mediation dialogue moving forward.

When using the skill of immediacy, the mediator leaves the conversation at hand to respond to something that has just occurred – perhaps a strong, non-verbal reaction or loud outburst. Focusing on the here and now requires that the mediator acknowledge and then name what he or she saw or heard, followed by an inquiry into responses that might include anger, crying, loud retorts, or non-verbal expressions that indicate an intense reaction. Here are some examples of immediacy: "I can see how angry you are right now; what just happened to cause that?" "From your reaction it is clear that you are not OK with what he just offered; what did that offer say to you to make you react that way?" "It looks like this conversation is upsetting you; what would you like to do now given your reaction – take a break or keep going?" "Is there something else that would be helpful at this point?" "You both look rather despondent right now; what could we do now to make it feel like we are moving forward or that it is worth continuing?"

Confronting discrepancy

Confronting discrepancy is similar to the skill of immediacy in that it also involves three elements: noticing, describing, and questioning. But rather than focus on strong emotions and reactions, it responds to what appears to the mediator as discrepancies in the parties' words or actions, or discrepancies between the parties' stated goals and their actions or procrastination towards achieving their goals.

Mediators use confronting discrepancy with caution and sparingly, as it can be experienced as challenging or judgmental. Attention to tone of voice and sensitivity are both necessary when using this skill to ensure that the intended message is one of curiosity, not blame. Here are some examples: "This is the third time that I have heard you say that you really want to get this issue settled, yet whenever an offer is made you refuse to discuss it; what is blocking you from having this discussion?" "You say that you want to hear your daughter's view of the situation, but whenever she tries to explain it, you interrupt and accuse her of exaggerating. Clearly the two of you strongly disagree on what has been happening. It will be impossible for us to discuss both perspectives if you are unable to allow your daughter to finish speaking. What could we do to make it easier for you to hear what she has to say about the situation?" "You told us that you have been looking for part-time work for the past six months, yet now we hear that you have stopped looking. What has caused you to do that?"

Normalizing

There might be times in mediation when the parties express feelings of hopelessness or despair, as if they are the only ones ever to experience such difficulty or strong emotion. When emotions or expressions convey despondency, gloom, or pessimism, letting the party know that he or she is not the only one to have experienced those emotions by normalizing them is both appropriate and reassuring. However, if it is not done with sincerity, or if it is not based on the mediator's real experience, normalizing can minimize a party's experience, rather than support it. When using the skill of normalizing, both timing and context are important. Normalizing would sound like this: "It is normal to be feeling discouraged, even somewhat hopeless, at this point in mediation. Let me reassure you that, although it is hard going right now, you are making progress and it will get easier." Or, "In my experience, it is not uncommon to feel disheartened in situations where resolution seems impossible. Is there anything that would make it easier for you to hang in a bit longer?" Normalizing can also help to reduce the threat that the mediation session itself might be producing, and in this way it helps promote learning.

Temperature taking and asking for feedback

Both of the above strategies ask for the parties' feedback on how things are going or how they are feeling overall about the process. In this way the mediator obtains direct information, and does not have to guess at how the parties are doing. These strategies are also used to check in with a party when it appears something might have been misinterpreted or perceived differently from what the mediator intended. Asking for feedback and "taking the temperature" of the room are powerful ways to avoid misunderstanding and continuing down the wrong path. For example: "What is your reaction to my attempt to have you talk to each other directly, rather than through me?" Or, "In this last conversation, you both expressed strong emotions and placed yourselves in vulnerable positions. Are you good to keep going or do you need a break?"

Verbal supports

Verbal supports are used to let the parties know that the mediator understands *why* they feel a certain way, not *how* they feel. Knowing the difference is important, because we can never really know how others feel. The best the mediator can do is to make a link between how she or he might feel in a similar situation. When making this type of link, the mediator needs to ensure that attention is not diverted from the party speaking. The mediator also wants to let the party know that it is OK to feel as he or she does, and to ensure that the mediator's response does not unintentionally attach blame. The following are examples of blaming phrases turned into communication helpers or verbal supports. Rather than saying, "I know how you feel," the mediator might say, "I can understand how you might be feeling now." A phrase such as "That sure made you angry" would be replaced by "I can see how that interaction might make you angry." Or, "You are really not making much sense right now" is exchanged for "I am having trouble understanding your point."

It is common for people in conflict to make global statements such as "you always ..." "you never ..." "you are forever ..." Because they connote blame and accusation that lead to defend responses, mediators need to notice when a party is using such statements and ask the speaker to be specific about the behaviour or ask for an example of the behaviour. For instance: "What would be an example of a time when that happened?" "This happens a lot to you, so it would be helpful if you could be specific about times when it occurs."

Improving Your Communication Skills

Opening the doors to communication is the pathway the mediator uses to help the parties find ways to deal better with their differences, but its terrain is guaranteed to be difficult and rocky at times. For this reason, the mediator needs to be well prepared and competent in dealing with a range of communication problems and barriers. Employing the skills described in this chapter only in a mediation setting, however, will not likely make the mediator competent in their use. Instead they need to be practised, and then incorporated into everyday interactions. Good communication skills are life skills.

Although they might appear easy when you read about them in this book, in actual practice these skills are surprisingly hard to master. Partly this is because not many of us have been taught communication theory and practice formally, and we pick up "bad" habits as we progress through life. So we need to notice and then "unlearn" the communication patterns that block our ability to take on new ways of interacting. Below are some suggestions to help you become more proficient in using these skills.

- Ask a friend to give you feedback as you practise listening for understanding and asking non-judgmental, curious questions.
- Watch your favourite TV or soap program. See if you can name the kinds of communication patterns you are observing: are the

questions open, closed, non-judgmental, consequential, empowering, and so forth? How well do the actors listen to each other? How can you tell? What could they do differently to be better listeners?

- Tape a TV soap program or good mystery movie. Watch it, stop the tape, then use an appropriate skill to listen for understanding (restating, reflecting, paraphrasing, summarizing). Continue starting and stopping the program until you have an opportunity to ask a bridging question, link or delink a threat-to-care, paraphrase, summarize, and so on. Record yourself responding, then go back and listen.
- Form a peer practice group or join an existing group in which you can practise your communication skills and receive feedback from others.
- Tape yourself mediating or facilitating a difficult conversation. Then go back and analyse your strengths and challenges. Reflect on what you would do differently in the future. Ask a more experienced person to review the tape with you and give you some feedback from his or her perspective. As you progress with your skills, review the tape from time to time to observe your progress – give yourself a pat on the back when you deserve it.
- Contact those who have trained you and ask if there are opportunities for internships, mentorship, co-mediation, or other relationships that would give you the opportunity to engage in reflective practice.

Having examined the theory, skills, strategies, and processes of insight mediation, the following chapter takes us in a different direction. It looks at recent achievements and future hopes for the insight approach from the perspective of three esteemed scholar-practitioners: Dr Andrea Bartoli, from Seton Hall University in South Orange, New Jersey; Dr Kenneth Melchin, from Saint Paul University in Ottawa; and Dr Jamie Price, from George Mason University in Washington, DC. Their knowledge and experience provide a fitting closure to the book, and I am most grateful for their insights.

Chapter Seven

The Insight Approach to Conflict:
Recent Achievements and Future Hopes

KENNETH MELCHIN, ANDREA BARTOLI,
AND JAMES PRICE

In the chapters of this book, Cheryl Picard offers theorists and practitioners a novel and exciting approach to the study and practice of interpersonal conflict mediation. When our book, *Transforming Conflict through Insight,* was first published, it would have been difficult to imagine the interest it would attract or the developments that would follow. Picard's book offers a mature presentation of developments she has pursued in the teaching and practice of insight mediation. We congratulate her on the leadership and guidance she continues to exercise in the field.

In this final chapter, we are pleased to offer readers a sketch of three new lines of analysis and practice that carry forward and transpose some of the central features of the insight approach to conflict. Based on the insight theory of Lonergan, and as Cheryl has been telling us throughout this book, insight mediation is a learning-centred approach that understands conflict as an occasion for insights that transform threat-defend patterns of interaction, disrupt stances of certainty, and open up horizons of curiosity among parties. In this chapter we explore the insight approach to conflict in three broader and more diverse fields of experience: retaliatory violence, spirituality, and genocide. The first and third of these are fields where conflicts typically become hardened and rooted deeply in community attitudes and convictions, with devastating consequences. The second is a field of application where spiritual traditions build on insight theory to offer resources for transforming conflicts in directions towards transformational learning and community healing.

The first section is written by Dr James Price, Director of the Sargent Shriver Peace Institute at George Mason University. In a project of the

Shriver Peace Institute, funded by the Bureau of Justice Assistance in the US Department of Justice, Price draws on core elements of the insight approach to conflict, and transposes them to contexts where police officers in Lowell, Massachusetts, and Memphis, Tennessee, are trained to respond creatively and constructively to situations of retaliatory violence. People living in communities of poverty frequently feel they have little reason to trust or cooperate with police. Consequently, when they are victimized by others, they see no other recourse than to take the law into their own hands. Crimes of retaliatory violence are now a major problem in American communities, and analysts argue that reversing the crisis requires interventions that transform people's experiences of social conflict and restore attitudes of trust and cooperation towards police. The Shriver Peace Institute project develops strategies for such interventions, and Price argues for the power and significance of the insight approach in the community healing that is needed in situations of retaliatory violence.

The second section is written by Dr Kenneth Melchin, Director of the Lonergan Centre at Saint Paul University, Ottawa. Typically, religion is viewed as a significant source of social conflict. Melchin, however, argues that spiritual traditions can offer resources for responding creatively and constructively to conflict. He draws on the insight approach to conflict to frame the inquiry, and asks how spirituality can function positively to help parties delink threats and shift from intransigence to openness in conflicts. His focus is the role of certainty in conflicts. Typically, religions are characterized as sources of certainty that exacerbate conflict. Yet, central to the Christian tradition are religious insights and practices that invite us to let go of certainty and become curious in new ways. He explores the link between faith in transcendent mystery and openness to uncertainty in world affairs, and offers a framework for investigating how diverse spiritual traditions could link with insight analysis to offer resources for healing conflicts in diverse contexts.

The third section is written by Dr Andrea Bartoli, Dean of the School of Diplomacy and International Relations at Seton Hall University, South Orange, New Jersey, and former dean of the School for Conflict Analysis and Resolution at George Mason University. His focus is genocide prevention, and his analysis explores ways the insight approach to conflict can help us think and act more responsibly in the face of perceived threats that exacerbate international relations and contribute to spiralling threat-defend convictions and behaviours at the core of genocides. His analysis highlights the role of meaning making in conflicts and the possibilities for new learning that can open up when events are understood as amenable to human meaning and responsible choosing. He concludes with reflections on a collective learning that can be discerned in recent decades in international relations. The insight approach to conflict champions the significance of this longer-term learning, and signals opportunities for leadership that can be exercised in steering this learning towards institutionalized cooperation on a global scale.

Sargent Shriver, Insight Skills, and Retaliatory Violence (by James Price)

I have had the pleasure of working with Cheryl Picard in recent years on the development of the insight approach to conflict analysis and resolution. But, unlike her, I am not a mediator. I direct the Sargent Shriver Peace Institute, and Sargent Shriver was not a mediator, either. He was, however, arguably the most effective and visionary American peace builder in the post–Second World War era. He created the Peace Corps, Legal Services for the Poor, Community Action, Head Start, No First Strike, and a host of other politically and socially innovative responses to the Cold War, racial conflict, poverty, and America's nuclear arms race with the former Soviet Union. So, although I am keenly interested in the skill set that the insight mediators trained at Carleton University employ to understand and resolve largely interpersonal and small group conflicts, I have become even more keen to answer a related question: How might it be possible to transpose insight skills that have been pioneered and developed in the field of mediation to the arenas of conflict that engaged Sargent Shriver? These are deep-rooted, often violent, structural conflicts that divide communities and societies on the basis of income, race, culture, and religion.

Recently, I have had a chance to wrestle with this question while working on a social conflict of central importance to Sargent Shriver when he was creating Legal Services for the Poor: the social conflict that is precipitated when laws and the enforcement of laws are perceived as oppressive and unjust by the people who are governed by them. Shriver viewed this conflict as "a crisis in the rule of law," and he addressed the problem in a speech to the Illinois State Bar Association in June 1966, less than a month after the American Bar Association committed to work with Shriver to spread the Legal Services Program to every state in the nation. As Shriver expressed the goal, "We're working for a day when a policeman, an official, a representative of law and order is not perceived as the enemy – as the source of danger and symbol of oppression" (Shriver 1966).

Alas, we are still working for that day. Today, in fact, the crisis in the rule of law that Shriver addressed is manifest in a more violent form. It is evident in the decisions people make – particularly people living in poor communities who feel they have little reason to trust the police or to cooperate with them – to take the law into their own hands by using violence to settle their conflicts with one another, or by covering up for those who do. Crimes of retaliatory violence are a major law enforcement problem in the United States today, but Shriver's assessment of the problem remains valid. To reverse the crisis in the rule of law, we must transform the social conflict between community members and the representatives of the law. To do that, Shriver said, "We have to alter – most basically – the perceptions of both children and adults. But we cannot alter perceptions unless we alter people's experiences."

How? Shriver sought to alter people's experiences of the law by creating Legal Services for the Poor, a program designed to provide people living in poverty with legal assistance in civil matters. That legacy lives on in the Legal Services Corporation and at the Sargent Shriver National Center on Poverty Law in Chicago. But how should we address the contemporary problem of violent retaliatory crime? It is in wrestling with the answer to this question that the insight approach to conflict resolution becomes relevant.

What if – in addition to their customary law enforcement skills and practices – police officers learned a specially adapted set of insight conflict-resolution and communication skills? Might they then be able to mitigate or even prevent this violent, tit-for-tat conflict behaviour? My suggested answer to that question is "yes," and a demonstration grant from the Bureau of Justice Assistance in the US. Department of Justice has given me and my colleagues in the School for Conflict Analysis and Resolution at George Mason University the opportunity to work with the police departments in Lowell, Massachusetts, and Memphis, Tennessee, to show why this could be so.

Retaliatory violence is a crime that occurs when conflict between individuals or groups spirals out of control. It occurs when community members decide that the best way to right a perceived wrong is to take justice into their own hands and resort to violence. As national Federal Bureau of Investigation statistics make clear, retaliatory violence is a chronic law enforcement problem that disproportionately affects the young and all too often turns lethal. In 2011, 75 per cent of homicides were precipitated by arguments or gang activity (United States 2011, table 10). Young people between the ages of thirteen and twenty-four made up 29 per cent of homicide victims (United States 2011, table 2) and 50 per cent of the victims of assault who suffered non-fatal gun injuries (United States 2015).

As a criminal act, retaliatory violence is the outward manifestation of interpersonal conflicts between individuals and groups engaged in violent, tit-for-tat patterns of retaliation. These cycles are extraordinarily difficult to disrupt, both for the individuals caught up in them and for the police officers whose job it is to disrupt them. Acts of retaliatory violence invariably place police officers in a reactive mode, leaving them both to manage the after-effects of a violent crime and wondering when and where the next shoe will drop. And as every officer knows, little progress on either front is possible without the active cooperation of the community.

On the community level, then, ongoing cycles of retaliatory·violence signal the existence of a broader social conflict between community and police over the legitimacy of police power and authority. As a report commissioned by the Bureau of Justice Statistics demonstrates, the principal manifestation of this conflict lies in the decisions of community members not to cooperate with the police, but to seek justice on their own terms instead. In the five years from 2006 to 2010, 52 per cent of violent crimes went unreported to the police, 34 per cent of cases went unreported because victims decided to deal with the problem themselves, and another 16 per cent went unreported because victims felt police either could not or would not help them (Langton et al. 2012).

A recent study by the International Chiefs of Police on the public image of police confirms Shriver's diagnosis of the problem. According to the study, the primary factor in determining whether or not community members will be inclined to cooperate with the police is public perception of fairness in policing. The study reveals that people tend to regard the exercise of police powers in their community as legitimate when they perceive the enforcement of the law to be fair, and when they perceive police officers to be committed to exercising their policing authority fairly and responsibly. The study also shows the correlation between police legitimacy and fairness holds constant for those who are being prosecuted and held accountable to the law, as well as those who are being protected by it (Gallagher et al. 2001).

Thus, retaliatory violence and police legitimacy are properly understood as mutually reinforcing, linked conflicts. For when the legitimacy of the power and authority of the police is in doubt, community
members take justice into their own hands and do not cooperate with
police officers. And when community members do not cooperate, it
becomes extremely difficult for police officers to investigate and close
existing cases of retaliatory violence, let alone to predict and prevent
the next ones. When violent, retaliatory crime goes unchecked, the rule
of law in the community declines and police legitimacy is further un-
dermined. In the extreme, attitudes emerge such as the one expressed
by a community member in one of Lowell's distressed areas: "The police just aren't there for us. They'd rather see us shoot each other and
then send the ambulance."[1] As Shriver clearly understood, in communities where levels of retaliatory violent crime are high, community
perceptions of police legitimacy tend to be especially low (see Butler
2009; Kubrin and Weitzer 2003). How might insight skills help to alter
the experiences that lead to these perceptions of police legitimacy and
interpretations of dire outcomes in relation to contact with the police?
How might these skills shift the perception of police as "villain" to
police as "defender"?

The relevance of insight skills to the deep-rooted problem of police
legitimacy and retaliatory violence is illustrated by a recent incident in
Lowell, during which five people were shot in a drive-by incident while
relaxing on their front porch. According to the detectives who investi-
gated the scene, the victims were some of the most uncooperative they
had encountered in their careers. One woman who was shot in her
shoulder and in both of her legs screamed at the firefighters and emer-
gency medical technicians helping her to leave her alone.

Clearly, if the goal of the police officers was to collect the evidence
and information they needed to solve the crime and punish the perpetrators, they were stymied by the non-cooperation of the victims. But if
their goal was also to understand and transform the conflict situation
operative at the crime scene, they had plenty to work with, and from a
law enforcement perspective every reason to do so. In all likelihood the
woman shot in the shoulder and the legs either knew or had observed

---

1 Interview with Lowell community member, Retaliatory Violence Insight Project,
   30 July 2012.

something that could lead police officers to identity the shooters and bring them to justice. So, the first step to solving that violent crime, to getting the shooter off the street, and to disrupting the pattern of retaliatory violence, would be to understand and resolve the woman's conflict with the police and the first responders – a conflict manifest in her decision not to talk to or cooperate with any of them.

The purpose of "insight policing" is to enable police officers to understand and to respond constructively to the resistance, non-cooperation, and other conflict behaviour they experience from community members. For example, three of the Memphis police officers we trained in insight policing skills were called to respond to a shooting. When they arrived at the scene, they found a group of young men congregated at the back of a house that had received multiple hits in a drive-by shooting. The young men did not want to talk to them. The officers reported that, if had they followed their customary law enforcement procedures, they would have handcuffed the young men and taken them to the police station for possible booking on gang-related activity. Their goal in handling the situation this way would have been twofold: on the one hand, to try to coax some useful information about the crime from the young men, and on the other, to keep them temporarily off the streets and unable to retaliate.

Instead, however, the officers remained at the scene with the young men and responded to their recalcitrance by asking a series of targeted broadening questions aimed at deepening their understanding of the situation from the men's perspective. By doing so they would be able to make decisions and act in ways that would include law enforcement and offer other potential help to the community. These officers understood the subtle but important difference between asking questions designed to solve a crime – questions that are closed in nature and interpreted as attacking and blaming, and asking questions that are open, genuinely curious, and designed to address the latent conflict between community members and police officers. They began by asking questions aimed at getting the information they needed to solve the crime: "What did you see?" "What can you tell us about the shooting?" "Who do you think might have done this?"

It did not take the officers long to learn that the young men had decided to stonewall them and that, as a result, they faced a decision of their own. How were they going to respond to this repudiation of their authority as officers of the law? I tend to think of these moments of split-second decision and action as "Shriver crossroads," because there are fundamentally two ways the officers could go. They could draw upon the power vested in them as law enforcement officers and decide to take the young men into custody. Or they could decide to shift their investigative curiosity from discovering the details of the crime to understanding the conflict behaviour of the young men. On this particular evening, the officers took the second path. Rather than respond to the threat presented to them by the youths' non-compliance, they chose to take a learning approach by "listening to understand," paraphrasing, then verifying their interpretation of what was taking place: "So it seems you've decided the best thing to do here is to stonewall us about the shooting. Do we have that right?" Upon receiving wry confirmation of this interpretation, the officers pursued a line of open, curious questions aimed at discovering how the young men arrived at this decision: "What makes keeping information from us the best thing to do here?" "What are you thinking will happen if you talk to us?" "What are you hoping to achieve?"

These questions enabled the officers to be strategically curious about why the young men did not want to talk to them about the shooting. Momentarily setting aside their desire to solve the crime and apprehend the perpetrators, the officers sought instead to learn what was at stake for the young men in their decision not to cooperate. Resisting the temptation to assume they already knew everything they needed to know about these young men and what their motives might be, the officers sought to understand the dire futures these young men were hoping to avoid in their refusal to cooperate with the police – in other words, they sought to discover their threats-to-cares. The officers then followed up with questions that enabled the young men to become curious for themselves, about whether non-cooperation with the police was in fact the best way forward under the circumstances.

Anyone familiar with insight mediation will recognize here an adaption of the skills insight mediators employ when they begin to engage in what Picard and Jull (2011) call "deepening the conversation." But the officers on the scene were not engaged in mediation. They were engaged in their law enforcement duties as community police officers. They were attempting to establish the legitimacy of their authority as police officers with a group of young men who had their own reasons for doubting it. And they were doing so as part of their responsibility to solve a violent crime and disrupt a potentially retaliatory response.

Needless to say, to experience police officers rolling up on them in the aftermath of a drive-by shooting triggered feelings of threat in the

young men, and they spontaneously adopted a defended, uncooperative stance. However, to experience these same police officers being
curious about them in their own terms confounded the expectations of
these young men and altered their perception of the officers. In the
language of the insight approach, the young men were able to delink
their feelings of threat from this encounter with the officers. This, in
turn, freed them to consider a wider range of possible responses to the
officers, including a re-evaluation of their original decision not to cooperate with them.

Indeed, the officers reported that, during the course of their encounter,
the young men volunteered information about the shooting that enabled
the officers to apprehend the shooter later that evening. That evening in
Memphis was the kind of day Sargent Shriver was working for.

Insight, Conflict, and Spirituality (by Kenneth Melchin)

Insight mediation seems to have set in motion a rather interesting array
of initiatives. Since the publication of *Transforming Conflict through
Insight*, my own research has centred on issues arising at the intersec-
tion of spirituality and ethics (see, for example, Melchin 2012). The following pages offer an opportunity to explore questions on spirituality
and conflict that began arising as Cheryl and I wrote *Transforming
Conflict through Insight*. At the time, these questions had to be put aside
until later, and I am pleased that "later" has arrived.

My question is: How can spirituality function positively to help parties shift from intransigence to openness in conflicts? My focus is on the
Christian tradition – in particular, that stream of Christianity that
shaped Bernard Lonergan, the author of *Insight*. Yet, I suggest that this
tradition provides resources that could be transposed to other contexts
that welcome women and men from diverse religious and secular belief
traditions.

Framed in terms of the insight approach, the challenge of conflict
arises because parties in conflict feel that things they value are threatened. When threatened, our natural curiosity about the cares of others
shuts down. Our focus is on defending from the perceived attack. The
threat narrative that shapes our thinking and feeling situates the actions of others within a rigid framework that links past memories and
present experiences to expectations of future harm. The effect of this
threat narrative is to create convictions about future harm. And central
to these convictions is our certainty this will indeed happen.

Of course, the problem with conflicts is that the longer a conflict goes on, the more evidence the parties provide for each other that these expectations are valid and our certainty is justified. Both parties operate from these convictions of expected harm, both have past histories that provide grounds for these expectations, both respond with gestures of defence, and these gestures never cease to provide compelling evidence that expectations of certain harm are indeed reasonable.

Resolving conflicts requires interventions, either by the parties themselves or by others, that dislodge the certainty of these expectations. When a breakthrough does occur, the insight approach to conflict explains it as a change, in at least one party, from certainty to uncertainty in the expectations about harm coming to something she cares about. Something – some word, some statement, some explanation, some gesture – evokes a different response, a response of curiosity about something unknown, rather than certainty about something presumed known. Often what triggers the new response is a discovery or admission that something was misinterpreted, misconstrued, mistaken. The solid chain of evidence bolstering certainty begins to reveal a gap. Initial responses are often cautious. Yet they reveal something new, something previously absent. This something new gives rise to a question: "If that isn't what you meant, then what did you mean?" "If that isn't what you were doing to me, then what were you doing?" Sometimes the question is too fragile to say aloud. What is important is that something new arises in consciousness, and this "something new" is an initial departure from certainty towards uncertainty and curiosity. Experienced mediators understand the importance of these moments, and seek to cultivate them in directions towards more open conversations.

I would like to explore what happens when spirituality provides resources for this move from certainty to uncertainty in conflicts. This might seem an odd thing to say, since most commentators portray spirituality, particularly when it is linked to established religions, as problematic precisely because it enforces certainty. Yet I argue there can be a form of certainty provided by spirituality where the effect is to foster openness to uncertainty in a wide range of human affairs.

Those familiar with mainstream Catholic and Protestant traditions know that Christians can never be certain that we understand God. In fact, we are taught that we can never claim to understand God because the Divine is a mystery that can never be known fully by us. The Divine is forever beyond our capacity to comprehend. This idea of God as transcendent mystery might seem plausible, but it also has implications for our knowledge of human life. We live in society and history, and throughout our lives we seek to understand the meaning of human existence. This search is a good thing. But, for Christians, this pursuit is ultimately the pursuit of transcendent mystery. This means that the ultimate meaning of historical existence does not lie within our grasp. Ultimates or absolutes in human life remain forever under a shroud of mystery (see, for example, Hughes 2003).

Yet Christians believe we can know something about the Divine. We can know that this mysterious God is a loving God, that the created universe is friendly because it is a gesture of this love, and that human life has an inalienable dignity because we participate in some special way in this mystery of Divine love. So there is a kind of certainty that is experienced in Christian life. Yet this is not a certainty about concrete outcomes in life, nor is it a certainty about the ultimate meaning of anything particular in life. Quite the opposite. One of the most important imperatives for a Christian is never to turn anything proximate or concrete into an ultimate. This would be idolatry. Only God is ultimate. This applies to things, objects, goals, and rules, but it also applies to expected outcomes, hoped-for events, and longed-for goals. It also applies to the things we fear. These too shall pass. Most important, it applies to expectations of fulfilment. To live fully as a Christian requires abandoning our frantic pursuit of this-worldly things to fulfil us. No thing can fulfil us, only God.

Christian faith, understood in this tradition, invites us to be quite deliberate in holding fast to this odd combination of certainty about Divine mystery and uncertainty about finding ultimate meaning in worldly things. We can let go of certainty about a lot of things in life precisely because we remain certain that God remains faithful to us. Through the centuries, Christian communities have developed diverse spiritual practices for living out this curious combination of certainty about Divine mystery and uncertainty about ultimate meanings in concrete life. A common feature of such spiritualities is the focus on new habits for thinking and living in ordinary situations. For example, many spiritual traditions teach participants new habits for living intensely in the moment and noticing out-of-the-ordinary features of ordinary things (see, for example, Gutiérrez 1984, esp. part two). Participants are taught to expect to be surprised by ordinary events and things. This is because the ordinary is never merely ordinary; it is also an occasion for encounter with Divine mystery. Participants practise expecting to "see God in all things."

Central to this spirituality is the difficult work of "letting go," and this involves letting go of certainty. Normally we greet ordinary events with this-worldly expectations because we are certain about them, we know what to expect. But living spiritually requires giving ourselves over to a possible surprise encounter with Divine mystery in the ordinary. To do this we need to let go and become uncertain about the meaning of what we are experiencing. In doing so, we open ourselves to a new curiosity, a new engagement with the ordinary that expects new meaning. To be sure, this involves skills for navigating considerable emotional turbulence, because frequently our confidence in life is rooted in expectations of certainty. Yet practitioners are taught these skills, and the result is that emotional turbulence can indeed be navigated successfully.

So how does all this relate to conflict? According to the insight approach, conflicts are experiences in which patterns of meaning have become all too familiar. They are driven by the certainty of our expectations of threats-to-cares, and they are resolved when parties delink from this certainty and become curious about the meanings of actions and values of others. I suggest that a Christian spiritual practice could be adapted to help prepare parties in conflict for this delinking from certainty and opening up to new meaning. The core of the Christian's response in such situations would be a cultivated openness to a transformative encounter with Divine mystery in the midst of conflict. The effect would be to remind the parties that ultimate certainties need never be linked to concrete life objects and experiences. Our total selves are never threatened in conflict because the ultimate meaning and value of our lives are rooted, not in worldly objects and events, but in transcendent mystery.

Such a spirituality would involve practices and habits for expecting transformative experiences amidst the emotional turbulence of conflict. Spiritual mentors would help participants cultivate practices for opening themselves to such experiences and greeting them as trustworthy, as encounters with Divine mystery. Our certainty about the Divine as loving grounds this confidence and helps give ourselves over to uncertainty and curiosity about the meanings and actions of others in conflict. The emotional turbulence of conflict does not go away. But spiritual practices help navigate the turbulence, with the expectation of encountering something significant in its midst.

At present, what is proposed is a hypothesis about a possible spiritual practice that could help participants in conflict achieve some of the goals that are anticipated by the insight approach. I believe that various Christian spiritual traditions – for example, the Benedictine or Ignatian – might have resources that could be adapted for conflict contexts. But I also believe the insight approach to conflict has important ingredients of its own to offer such a spiritual practice. These include a framework for understanding conflict, insights into the role of certainty about threats-to-cares in sustaining conflicts, and insights into the role of uncertainty and curiosity in delinking threats-to-cares and opening avenues for resolution.

Moreover, similar resources might also be found in other religious and secular belief traditions. Bernard Lonergan's study of the operations of human consciousness provides a framework for understanding a basic structure to transformative experience that can be expected in all fields of human life and all traditions. Indeed, his analysis leads us to expect that such transformative experiences occur all the time and that the task of scholars of religion is to identify, understand, and affirm them whenever and wherever they occur.

Finally, I would add, in the spirit of Lonergan's invitation to self appropriation, that this analysis of spiritual resources for conflict also leads us to examine the self-understanding of experienced insight mediators.

Insight mediators are trained to expect uncertainty and surprise in conflict. They are trained to help parties in conflict stay in uncertainty, probe uncertainty, and resist the comfort zones provided by certainty about the meanings and actions of others. Their training helps parties become uncertain and curious about their own cares and threats-to-cares. To do this, insight mediators draw upon a discipline and self-possession whose analysis might well prove central in elaborating a spirituality for conflict. My effort has been to suggest that scholarship on conflict and spirituality could prove helpful in identifying how, contrary to popular expectations, spiritual traditions could operate positively to enhance learning amidst the turbulence of conflicts.

The Insight Approach: Applications to Violence and Genocide (by Andrea Bartoli)

Large and powerful human systems have been built to confront threats. The plausibility of a nuclear attack is still driving an extremely high level of investment dedicated to defending countries from enemies. However, all these activities are bound to the security dilemma:

whatever a state is investing in defence can be interpreted by an adversary as aggressive and threatening. But what is a threat? And how can we approach perceived threats in ways that avoid exacerbating the spiral of threat and violence. I want to suggest some ways the insight approach to conflict can help us think and act more responsibly in face of perceived threats in international relations.

Any threat is perceived relationally. Tetsushi Ogata, while working on the socialization of threats, aptly observes that, in order to be effective, a threat must be recognized "as such" by the receiver.[2] Many authors have observed that threats of punishment that are never carried out lose their deterrence capacity. A "threat," in order to be effective, must be believed. But what about the paradox of the security dilemma? What about actions that are not intended as threats by their authors but are perceived as such? The effects of "attributed threats" are all around us, from Soviet-American relations to the killing fields of Pol Pot in Cambodia. In such situations we encounter threats that are attributed by the receiver, and these frequently become the basis for new destructive responses.

The insight approach invites the conversational dimension of meaning and learning into discussions of international security. Bernard Lonergan famously wrote: "Objectivity is the fruit of authentic subjectivity." A threat is never exclusively and deterministically objective, something that exists outside ourselves over which we have no control. A threat is not something that simply overwhelms us without any room for us to respond. Humans can be creative in the midst of violence. Humans can be wise in front of threatening folly. Humans can be courageously apt in the face of others who are systematically violating bodies, rights, and lives. Humans can learn and humans can choose. This learning and choosing, in many ways, is what differentiates us from animals. The response to a threat is not scripted in our instincts, in our genes, in our habits. It is constructed through the meaning that we attribute to situations. Making meaning is the sacred responsibility of each of us, especially while facing violent threats, systematic exclusions, and hate language.

---

2 Ogata is in the final stages of his doctoral dissertation on "The Socialization of Threats in Mass Killing," to be defended at the School for Conflict Analysis and Resolution, George Mason University.

The problem reaches extraordinary proportion with genocide. Genocide is not an accident. It is not an occasional riot. It is not a trivial mistake. It is the result of many choosing to exclude, violate, and oppress while many others choose indifference. Genocide is not possible in a legitimate, representative, and inclusive political system. A functioning state would have all the means to intervene and stop the incitement, the initial criminal acts, and often the gathering of destructive groups. Genocide is made possible by the choices of many interpreting the difference of others (ethnic, religious, national) as a threat. It is also made possible by the indifference of others who do not prevent the victimization of the targeted party. Genocide is highly relational. It is constructed around a meaning that claims a false certainty, attributes guilt, removes self-responsibility, and is backed by force.

In the middle of genocides we have encountered the rescuers: the people who risk their lives to help others, save others, liberate others. The rescuers demonstrate that, even in the midst of the most egregiously violating environments, humans can choose, we can let understanding liberate ourselves and others. What the rescuers do, as the martyrs, as the artists, as any creative human, is to call everyone in the situation (and everyone who happens to encounter them later through testimonies) to a different relational space: something else is possible. A new word is possible. A new choice is possible.

The insight approach to conflict highlights the possibilities for openings, new meanings, learning, and surprise in areas that many consider hopeless. It reminds us that making meaning is what we do as humans, that we do so conversationally, that we can invite each other to be attentive, intelligent, reasonable, and responsible. It also calls us to engage conversationally when we see breaches in our personal and collective attentiveness, when we do not pay attention to data properly, when we make our decisions based on biases, rather than on evidence, when we are unreasonable and irresponsible. The insight approach does not prescribe a formula, but simply invites us to consider the responsibility of being and becoming fully human even in the midst of extraordinarily challenging environments. If this is true in extreme cases, then what can happen in times when tensions are less violent and destructive? New challenges can become the theatre of new possibilities, and creativity and communication can be our response to pressing and oppressing problems.

This book by Cheryl Picard is an invitation to explore the role of creativity, communication, learning, and choosing in conflict. At the core of the insight approach is the focus on learning and choosing, both in the construction of conflict and in its resolution. As a human family, we must choose paths of individual and collective discernment that peace entails, especially through the prism of local, national, and international responsibilities. There are many areas where member states have been collaborating for a long time, and we have learned a great deal through these experiences. Unfortunately, genocide prevention is not one of them. The awareness that this massive loss of human lives should be prevented and punished is relatively recent. Historically, the United Nations has been at the forefront of the process, first with the International Convention of 1948 and then with the creation of the role of the Special Adviser for the Prevention of Genocide in 2004, ten years after the genocide in Rwanda.

We are learning. And the insight approach to conflict invites us to focus on this learning as we appropriate the fruits of past experiences in international affairs. The case of post-election violence in Kenya demonstrates that we can learn collectively even from horrendous cases. The spectre of genocide was present during the crisis and beyond. Yet we now see enormously creative and institutional improvements. The International Conference of the Great Lakes Region has been at the forefront. The next effort will need to address issues of coordination among local, national, regional, and international levels. The Office of the Special Adviser on Genocide Prevention has contributed with its Framework of Analyses and Training. Many other instances of the UN system have contributed as well, starting with the Special Adviser on the Responsibility to Protect.

Collective learning from past experience is key to continued success. Experience seems to tell us that emerging norms are strengthened when they are expressions of self-regulation of individual states and of collaborative configurations. Insight analysis would suggest that this is because parties themselves are engaged in the learning and choosing. Norms and practices are learned over time. The United Nations system was not constructed in a day, and it is actually still in the making. When norms are institutionalized, they promote the learning of patterns of cooperation that allow the process of self-organizing by member states.

A fundamental prevention orientation is embedded in state-citizen relations, and this is fundamental to how parties learn about their mutual relations and their external obligations. This process is also far from complete, and it is manifested in how states do or do not fulfil their duties. Each case is an opportunity for current arrangements to prove themselves in the context of collective learning. Each is a unique situation, but each provides opportunities for new learning and occasions for advancing collective learning. In this context, failures are extremely important because they provide the critical lens necessary for improvement.

Each human situation is by definition unique, in the same way that each person is unique. Yet our learning finds expressions of universality in individual cases. Each individual person is unique, yet each is the holder of inherent rights that must be recognized universally. Similarly, each situation is unique, yet each must be interpreted as an expression of universal values. Genocide prevention attempts to offer its framework as a fundamental component of the UN member states' self-understanding. The UN system has contributed to this learning trajectory, linking norms and institutions, and serving the world through its own learning.

Another insight is that universal mechanisms are simply expressions of nation-states' political will, and that they do not have political capacities and roles independently of the states that must implement them. To realize them, member states need to learn and choose them. The emergence of new positions, such as the Special Advisers on Genocide Prevention and on Responsibility to Protect, allow the expression of political will by member states over time in a way that potentially could lead towards more concerted strategies. Many regions are moving towards further continental integration, so they can speak with one voice, and towards further diversification, so local communities can have greater influence. Both tendencies play important roles in advancing the prevention approach to genocide, war crimes, crimes against humanity, and ethnic cleansing.

Among the most important forms of learning are those involving past violence. Violent episodes that point to current and past experiences of harm are rich repositories of extremely delicate memories and responsibilities. When violence occurs, its impact stays with human communities for centuries. It is essential for states to devote significant resources to address the past, to learn from the past, to make sure the past is understood accurately, to respect the memory of peoples and events, and to enable multiple actors to have collective conversations about shared experiences. They need to construct inclusive narratives that make the recurrence of past crimes less probable in current and future events. When member states play leadership roles in this learning of past narratives, current values, and future opportunities for cooperation, they become able to execute an adaptable architecture for institutionalized cooperation and collective learning.

The insight approach to conflict comes to us at an important time, a time that is ripe for collective learning. Of the more than seven billion people in our world today, for the first time in history it is accepted and expected that each and every individual will go to school, will learn to read and write. Today's technology has made it possible for us to learn in a way that was unimaginable to our ancestors. We can be present to one another. We can enter into one another's lives. A vast cultural release of human creativity is in process, and we can claim as "ours" the concerns of other humans on other continents. We now have universal languages of human rights to express our concerns for others, and institutions such as the United Nations to help actualize them. The magnificence of human genius is being revealed to us, and the hope of making our world truly fit for human dignity is a surging, valid, wise, and valuable dream. The invitation of learning is central to this dream, and it is extended to all. We believe the insight approach invites us to follow this invitation into a hopeful engagement of learning that we can expect to encounter amidst the difficult conflicts that challenge our collective living.

In Conclusion

At the centre of the insight approach to conflict stands a set of core ideas about conflict: threats-to-cares, conflict as constituted by relational meaning, defend patterns of interaction, and transformative learning. In the past decade, Cheryl Picard has developed an impressive range of skills based on the insight approach to train mediators to help parties shift from intransigence to openness in situations of conflict. In this final chapter, we have explored how these core ideas are being developed and transposed to new contexts where groups, communities, and nations struggle with the terrible human hardships imposed by intractable social conflicts.

We argue that the insight approach to conflict shows considerable promise. Mediators can be trained to help parties gain insights that delink threats and transform interpersonal conflicts. Police can be trained to intervene differently to open up novel possibilities for action in communities paralysed by retaliatory violence. Spiritual traditions can offer insights and practices for dislodging certainties at the core of conflicts. And international institutions can benefit from a collective learning

about the certainties and threat-defend convictions at the core of genocides. In each case, we can observe that, although conflicts are social
relationships, the critical controls for humanizing these relationships lie
in personal acts of meaning. Conflicts arise when the behaviours of others are interpreted, when these interpretations evoke feelings of threats-
to-cares, and when the personal horizons shaped by these feelings give
rise to meanings and responses that become the behaviours that get
interpreted by others as further threats-to-cares. Conflicts are social
schemes or circles of action-response linkages. Yet the events in these
social schemes are personal acts of meaning, and so they can be changed
in the direction of greater openness and responsibility.

The insight approach offers a framework for understanding how personal acts of meaning and responsibility can shift the direction of social
conflict schemes towards open and humanizing possibilities. We offer
these explorations of three novel applications of the insight approach in
the hope that they support and stimulate both the work of insight mediation and its development and transposition to new contexts. This
needs to engage researchers, but it also needs to engage practitioners
who will develop the skills and skills-training programs that implement the fruits of research. We are grateful for the collaboration that has
led to the recent achievements outlined in the chapters of this book.
And we look forward to the projects that advance the realization of future hopes.

An Example of a Mediator's Opening Comments

Thank you both for coming today. I know that talking to each other about things you feel strongly about and disagree on can be difficult; I admire each of you for being here. Although mediation is not easy, it very often does make people's lives better.

As a way to begin, and perhaps to settle us all down a bit, I'll take a few minutes to review some of the points from our individual discussions last week.

First, and very important, this is your process, and it will follow the path that you choose together. My role will be to help you talk to each other in a way that is productive and fair. I will do this by listening to understand what each of you is saying, and by exploring how what matters to you is threatened through your interactions. The aim is to help you discover new ways of interacting that will resolve your differences and make your lives better.

As your mediator,

- I will listen to what you have to say and ensure that I understand what you mean.
- I will also ensure that you understand each other by confirming that what was interpreted was intended.
- I will remain impartial by not judging your viewpoints or actions, and by not making decisions for you.
- Finally, I will ensure there is ample opportunity to say all that you need to say to each other.

With that in mind, I wonder if you have requests of each other or for me that would make it easier for you to talk about your feelings and what really matters to you in this situation.

[After waiting for the parties to respond, the mediator summarizes her understanding of the protocol to be used in the mediation. If appropriate she might offer a suggestion or two that in the past has helped to create a good atmosphere for dialogue.]

As I understand it, you have agreed to listen closely to each other and wait until each other is finished speaking before responding. I would add that it also helps to listen for new information that changes your perspective from the one you have now. If something occurs to you while the other person is talking, you can make a note of it on the paper I've provided so you don't forget bring it up when it is your turn to speak.

When we met last week I brought up the question of confidentiality. Let me go over that again to ensure that we all have the same understanding. First, I can assure you that I will hold what is said here in the strictest confidence. I have no obligation to report either the content or the results of our time together to anyone else. Furthermore, I have no reason to keep my notes after you make your decisions about how to resolve the situation between you. Do you have any questions about that?

Now, for you, what are your expectations regarding confidentiality? Do you need your discussions to remain within these four walls? Do you need the freedom to talk about any decisions reached with others?

You each agreed to stay for three hours today. Does that still work? I also asked you to block off an additional half-hour to give us some flexibility to go a bit longer if we feel that we are close to resolution. Are you OK with that, too?

There are just a few more points to go over before we begin. If an agreement is reached, do either of you need to check in with anyone prior to finalizing that agreement or are you in a position to make those decisions independently? And are you looking to put the decisions reached here today in writing or is there another way to ensure understanding and agreement? If you prefer a written outcome document, how will this happen?

Do either of you have anything to add that would make this a more comfortable or more meaningful experience? Do you have any questions? Are you ready to begin?

Transition to Phase 2

Let's begin with each of you talking about what it is that you are hoping will be changed for the better if you have a productive conversation here today.

Who would like to begin?

Some Tips for Holding a Caucus

When calling a caucus,
- have a specific purpose in mind;
- always caucus with both sides; if you are co-mediating, both mediators should caucus with each party;
- be aware of the length of time spent with each party, and do not leave one party alone for too long;
- clarify the issue of confidentiality in relation to the information shared in caucus, and be certain that you clarify with the party what is or is not to be kept confidential.

During the caucus,
- keep in mind your original goal for caucusing, and be focused yet flexible in seeking the information that would help the parties continue talking;
- emphasize strengths and offer positive feedback that might be more difficult to offer in joint session;
- before returning to the joint session, review what, if any, information is to be kept confidential.

After the caucus,
- choose an approach to open the joint session that best suits what you have learned and the feelings that were shared in the caucus;
- be discriminating about what is shared – judgment, timing, and respect for privacy are crucial to being able to convey your promise of impartiality and competency.

Remember, one of the main reasons to caucus is to uncover resistance to communication that is blocking the parties' ability to learn and change. Some other reasons you might decide to caucus include:

- to allow a breather or cooling-off period;
- to allow strong feelings to be expressed in private;
- to explore resistance more fully to discover concerns that might not yet have surfaced, allowing the parties to explain their position while not under each other's scrutiny;
- to reality check the parties' demands;
- to determine if there are mediator-party issues that should be addressed.

Mediators must maintain the parties' trust. Caucusing interferes with transparency and blocks the free flow of information and thoughts that are taking place in joint sessions. For this reason, private conversations between parties can lead one or both parties to wonder if the mediator is still impartial when joint sessions resume. This is why each side should receive an equal number of caucuses and why the mediator should keep each caucus to about the same length of time.

Sample "Consent to Participate in Mediation" Document

This "Consent to Participate in Mediation" is made between the mediator, *Cheryl Picard*, and each of the parties involved in the conflict situation: *Lynne Roberts* and *Samantha Edwards*. This agreement, which will be signed at the start of the mediation, indicates that Lynne Roberts and Samantha Edwards understand the process that will take place between them and the mediator. It also expresses their intent to make a serious attempt to the resolve the difficulties between them.

Both Lynne Roberts and Samantha Edwards agree to:
1. Engage in open, honest communication and to share all relevant information with the purpose of trying to resolve the difficulties between us.
2. Make known, should it happen, their wish to terminate the mediation before its completion in sufficient time for this decision to be discussed before leaving.
3. Take no new steps in any legal or formal administrative proceedings regarding the situation between them during the course of the mediation.
4. Not call our mediator, Cheryl Picard, as a witness in any subsequent legal or administrative proceedings. We also agree not to compel her to produce any notes or records from the mediation, and not to sue her personally.

As your mediator, I, Cheryl Picard:
1. Promise to assist each of you to talk about the difficulties between you in a safe and productive manner so that you can gain insight into the threats and defend responses creating these difficulties. I

will also help you to discover new and less threatening patterns of interactions, and to use these new insights to help you make decisions that you can each agree with.

2. Will not make decisions or impose my view. My role is to guide you in a learning conversation in which you can discuss your experience and understandings and change problematic interactions for the better.

3. Agree to keep all information shared during the mediation process strictly confidential except in accordance with the law. Because I also work as a university professor, I might wish to use the information from your mediation for research or educational purposes. If I were to do this, I promise to keep anonymous all names, departmental information, or any other identifying information.

In addition,

4. There might be times when I ask to meet with each of you privately to help move the learning conversation forward. Please feel free to ask to talk privately with me if needed.

5. If I determine that it is not possible to resolve the situation through mediation, I will suggest the process be terminated. If this should happen, I will discuss the reasons and suggest other possible options for dealing with the issues between you.

6. The mediation will be held at Carleton University in the Loeb Building, 4th floor, in Room D494, the "Mediation Learning Room," on October 22, 2014, beginning at 1:00 p.m. and possibly going until 5:00 p.m.

7. As discussed in the pre-mediation, you are asked to keep three hours open for the mediation, with the possibility of staying for an extra hour in the event that taking the extra time would be beneficial. This means that you agree to be available until 5:00 p.m. If additional mediation sessions are required, the decision to do this will be discussed and agreed to by you before closing the mediation session.

I, _____ consent to act as mediator in accordance with the above terms.
   (Cheryl Picard)

I, _____ and I, _____ have read,
   (Lynne Roberts)   *(Samantha Edwards)*

understood, and agree to the above ways of interacting in our mediation.

Dated at Carleton University in Ottawa on October 22, 2014.

Sample "Outcome Agreement"

As a result of mediation and with the intent to develop transparent, honest, and improved communication, I, *Lynne Roberts*, and I, *Samantha Edwards*, have made the following decisions. Our intentions through this agreement include equity and fairness of opportunities, along with a commitment to be transparent about our intentions towards each other and to check our assumptions in a timely and respectful manner.

With the understanding that this agreement focuses on future behaviour and interactions, we agree to undertake the following decisions immediately upon returning to work with the aim of improving the patterns of relations between us:

1. Lynne, as manager will demonstrate confidence in Samantha's abilities by giving her the first available opportunity to "act" as supervisor, and thereafter at reasonable intervals while also allowing opportunities for other team members to act in this position. These acting assignments are to carry on for significant periods of time such as would be the case when the manager takes annual leave, attends courses, or is away for a minimum of one or more successive weeks.
2. Samantha will acknowledge and accept Lynne's management decisions and consult with her in a professional and respectful manner on issues relevant to work assignments. When in disagreement with Lynn's management decisions, Samantha agrees to follow the accepted organizational chain of command, rather than speaking to others outside this organizational framework.
3. Lynne and Samantha will accept each other's differing work and communication styles by respectfully acknowledging each other's opinions and contributions when working together and in team

meetings, and by providing feedback to each other in a timely and professional manner. Each commits to keeping an open mind by staying curious and trying to look at the issues from the other's perspective and to allow opportunities for disagreement in a professional manner.

4. Samantha and Lynne commit to ensuring that actual or potential problems with each other are dealt with directly and in a timely and respectful way. When they appear to disagree, they will follow a process for checking things out that might include: making an appointment to see each other; thinking about the issue beforehand, rather than mentioning it in the moment; informing the other about the issue before the meeting so that both have an opportunity to think about it; advising each other about the urgency of dealing with the issue; discussing the issue in a timely fashion; meeting in person, rather than by e-mail; avoiding unnecessary documentation; not discussing the issue in front of others; and being open to being mistaken.

5. Lynne will support Samantha and provide her with opportunities for ongoing learning to further develop her supervisory and leadership skills within the team.

6. Samantha will fully participate in team meetings, staff meetings, and individual supervision meetings in an open and respectful manner.

7. Each of the above points of agreement is to be put into effect immediately. After a period of thirty days, Lynne and Samantha agree to meet in private to review how these actions are affecting their relations at work.

Both Lynne and Samantha acknowledge and agree that:

1. they fully understand the terms of this agreement;
2. all decisions made are reasonable;
3. they sign this agreement freely, voluntarily, and without duress;
4. they fully intend to abide by the decisions above, and they both acknowledge and agree that this document reflects their strong show of support for its fulfilment;
5. in the event that either Lynne or Samantha is not satisfied with the completion of what was agreed to, she agrees first to talk with the other party about her dissatisfaction, and if it cannot be resolved between them, they will return to mediation before any other recourse is taken;

6. should mediation fail to resolve the issues brought forward, pursu-
   ant to point 5, they agree to notify the Director of Human Resources
   in writing about the situation; both Lynne and Samantha will give
   serious consideration to any suggestions from the Director on how
   to resolve the matter before any other steps are taken to involve
   parties outside the department.

_____   _____

  Lynne Roberts   Samantha Edwards

Dated Ottawa, October 22, 2014.

Insight Mediator Self-assessment Tool

1. Understanding the Process of Insight Mediation and the Dynamics of Conflict

- What do I understand as the process and goal of insight mediation and my role in it?
- How well do I understand the concepts of learning, generating insights, meaning making, and interpretation?
- How would I define conflict to others?
- How able am I to convene a mediation session?
- How able am I to determine if a conflict situation is suitable for mediation?

2. Ability to Provide an Effective Insight Mediation Process

- How competent am I in each phase of the insight mediation process? Which phase is the most difficult and why?
- How do I plan to improve my abilities while working in this phase?
- How able am I to notice and help parties change their "defend" patterns of interaction?
- How able am I to encourage perspective taking between the parties?
- How able am I to stimulate a creative exploration of new ways of interacting that would reduce threats?
- How able am I to help the parties explore and evaluate the consequences of these new interactions?
- How able am I to summarize what the parties agree to, either in writing or in some other form?

3. Analytical and Responsive Intentionality Skills

- How able am I to understand the conflict situation and verify areas of threat?

- How able am I to think and act "with responsive intentionality"?
- How able am I to help the parties discover their threats-to-cares and at what level the cares are operating?
- How able am I to discover the meaning making that led to the parties' actions?
- How able am I to help the parties broaden their knowledge and understanding and surface the threats and defend responses that are contributing to the conflict?
- How able am I to deepen the learning conversation?
- How able am I to screen, retain, process, and synthesize information accurately and in the moment?
- How able am I to link the present with past experiences and expectations of an unwelcome or dire future?

4. Communication and Empathetic Skills

- How able am I to speak in a clear, direct, confident, and caring manner?
- How able am I to use the skills of listening to understand?
- How able am I to notice defend stories and avoid paraphrasing them?
- How able am I to ask curious and elicitive questions that uncover threats-to-cares and generate new insights?
- How able am I to verify that these insights are correct?
- How able am I to use deepening skills such as bridging, layering, finishing, and using?
- How comfortable am I with high emotion and using the skill of immediacy?
- How able am I to reflect emotions and deepen to discover what these feelings are about?
- How well do I understand the concept of feelings as carriers of values?
- How able am I to foster a relationship that is safe for the parties to express their emotions?

5. Overall Presence and Style as a Mediator

- How would I describe my personal style?
- How able am I to act with integrity, flexibility, and creativity?
- How able am I to be impartial and to demonstrate it to the parties?
- How able am I to provide a safe atmosphere in which to discuss threats-to-cares and defend responses?

- How able am I to instil confidence in mediation as a learning process?
- How confident am I to present myself in a way that demonstrates my ability as a mediator?
- Do I see myself working as a professional mediator in the future? If so, what do I see as my current limitations to working as a professional mediator?

References

Abdel Wahab, Mohamed S., Ethan Katsh, and Daniel Rainey. 2012. *Online Dispute Resolution: Theory and Practice: A Treatise on Technology and Dispute Resolution*. The Hague, Netherlands: Eleven International Publishing.

Bellah, Robert N., Richard Madsen, William M. Sullivan, Ann Swidler, and Steven M. Tipton. 1986. *Habits of the Heart: Individualism and Commitment in American Life*. Oakland: University of California Press.

Berger, Peter L., and Thomas Luckmann. 1966. *The Social Construction of Reality*. London: Penguin Books.

Bishop, Peter, Cheryl Picard, Rena Ramkay, and Neil Sargent. 2015. *The Art and Practice of Mediation*, 2nd ed. Toronto: Emond Montgomery.

Boulding, Kenneth E. 1962. *Conflict and Defense: A General Theory*. New York: Harper.

Burton, John. 1990a. *Conflict: Human Needs Theory*. New York: St Martin's Press.

Burton, John. 1990b. *Conflict: Resolution and Provention*. New York: St Martin's Press.

Bush, Robert A. Baruch, and Joseph P. Folger. 1994. *The Promise of Mediation: The Transformative Approach to Conflict*. San Francisco: Jossey-Bass.

Bush, Robert A. Baruch, and Joseph P. Folger. 2004. *The Promise of Mediation: The Transformative Approach to Conflict*, rev. ed. San Francisco: Jossey-Bass.

Butler, Paul. 2009. *Let's Get Free: A Hip Hop Theory of Justice*. New York: Free Press.

Canada. 1998. Status of Women Canada. *Family Mediation in Canada: Implications for Women's Equality*. Ottawa.

Canary, Daniel J., and Brian H. Spitzberg. 1990. "Attribution Biases and Associations between Conflict Strategies and Competence Outcomes." *Communications Monographs* 57 (2): 139–51.

Cloke, Kenneth. 2001. *Mediating Dangerously: The Frontiers of Conflict Resolution.* San Francisco: Jossey-Bass.

Coser, Lewis. 1968. *Continuities in the Study of Social Conflict.* New York: Free Press.

Deutsch, Morton. 1973. *The Resolution of Conflict: Constructive and Destructive Processes.* New Haven, CT: Yale University Press.

Dworkin, Ronald. 1977. *Taking Rights Seriously.* Cambridge, MA: Harvard University Press.

Etzioni, Amitai. 1993. *The Spirit of Community: Rights, Responsibilities, and the Communitarian Agenda.* New York: Crown.

Fisher, Roger, and William L. Ury. 1981. *Getting to Yes: Negotiating Agreement without Giving In.* Boston: Houghton Mifflin.

Folberg, Jay, and Alison Taylor. 1984. *A Comprehensive Guide to Resolving Conflicts without Litigation.* San Francisco: Jossey-Bass.

Gallagher, Catherine, Edward R. Maguire, Stephen D. Mastrofski, and Michael D. Reisig. 2001. *The Public Image of the Police: Final Report to the International Association of Chiefs of Police.* Washington, DC: George Mason University, Administration of Justice Program. Available online at http://www .theiacp.org/The-Public-Image-of-the-Police.

Goffman, Erving. 1974. *Frame Analysis: An Essay on the Organization of Experience.* Boston: Northeastern University Press.

Goldstein, Jeffrey. 1999. "Emergence as a Construct: History and Issues." *Emergence: A Journal of Complexity Issues in Organizations and Management* 1 (1): 49–72.

Gordon, Thomas. 1970. *Parent Effectiveness Training.* New York: Three Rivers Press.

Gordon, Thomas. 1974. *Teacher Effectiveness Training.* New York: Three Rivers Press.

Gordon, Thomas. 1977. *Leader Effectiveness Training.* New York: G.P. Putnam's Sons.

Gustavo Gutiérrez, Gustavo. 1984. *We Drink from Our Own Wells.* Trans. Matthew J. O'Connell. Maryknoll, NY: Orbis Books.

Heider, Fritz. 1958. *The Psychology of Interpersonal Relations.* Hillsdale, NJ: Lawrence Erlbaum Associates.

Himes Joseph. 1980. *The Nature of Social Conflict in Conflict and Conflict Management.* Athens: University of Georgia Press.

Hocker, Joyce, and William Wilmot. 1995. *Interpersonal Conflict.* Madison, WI: Brown and Benchmark.

Hoffman, David A. 2011. "Mediation and the Art of Shuttle Diplomacy." *Negotiation Journal* 27 (3): 263–309.

Hughes, Glen. 2003. *Transcendence and History*. Columbia: University of Missouri Press.

Jones, Tricia, and Ross Brinkert. 2008. *Conflict Coaching: Conflict Management Strategies and Skills for the Individual*. Thousand Oaks, CA: Sage.

Katsh, Ethan, and Janet Rifkin. 2001. *Online Dispute Resolution: Resolving Conflicts in Cyberspace*. San Francisco: Jossey-Bass.

Kauffman, Stuart A. 2008. *Reinventing the Sacred*. New York: Basic Books.

Kubrin, Charis E., and Ronald Weitzer. 2003. "Retaliatory Homicide: Concentrated Disadvantage and Neighborhood Culture." *Social Problems* 50 (2): 157–80.

Lang, Michael, and Alison Taylor. 2000. *The Making of a Mediator: Developing Artistry in Practice*. San Francisco: Jossey-Bass.

Langton, Lynn, Marcus Berzofsky, Christopher Krebs, and Hope Smiley-McDonald. 2012. "National Crime Victimization Survey: Victimizations Not Reported to the Police, 2006-2010." Washington, DC: US Department of Justice, Office of Justice Programs, Bureau of Justice Statistics. Available online at http://www.bjs.gov/content/pub/pdf/vnrp0610.pdf.

Lonergan, Bernard. [1957] 1992. *Collected Works of Bernard Lonergan*, vol. 3, *Insight: A Study of Human Understanding*. Toronto: University of Toronto Press.

Lonergan, Bernard. 1972. *Method in Theology*. New York: Herder and Herder.

Macfarlane, Julie. 1995. *Court-based Mediation for Civil Cases: An Evaluation of the Ontario Court (General Division) ADR Centre*. Toronto: Ministry of the Attorney General.

MacIntyre, Alasdair. 1981. *After Virtue: A Study in Moral Theory*. Notre Dame, IN: University of Notre Dame Press.

Maslow, Abraham. 1943. "A Theory of Human Motivation." *Psychological Review* 50 (4): 370–96.

Maslow, Abraham. 1954. *Motivation and Personality*. New York: Harper.

Matthews, B. Alex, and Fran H. Norris. 2002. "When Is Believing 'Seeing'? Hostile Attribution Bias as a Function of Self-reported Regression." *Journal of Applied Social Psychology* 32 (1): 1–32.

Mead, George Herbert. 1934. *Mind, Self, and Society*. Chicago: University of Chicago Press.

Melchin, Kenneth R. 2012. "Charity and Justice in Economic Life." *Theoforum* 43 (1–2): 135–52.

Melchin, Kenneth, and Cheryl Picard. 2008. *Transforming Conflict through Insight*. Toronto: University of Toronto Press.

Mezirow, Jack. 1990. *Fostering Critical Reflection in Adulthood: A Guide to Transformative and Emancipatory Learning*. San Francisco: Jossey-Bass.

Mezirow, Jack. 1991. *Transformative Dimensions of Adult Learning*. San Francisco: Jossey-Bass.

Mohr, Bernard J., and Jane M. Watkins. 2002. *The Essentials of Appreciative Inquiry: A Roadmap for Creating Positive Futures*. Waltham, MA: Pegasus Communications.

Moore, Christopher. 2003. *The Mediation Process: Practical Strategies for Resolving Conflict*. San Francisco: Jossey-Bass.

Nader, Laura. 1990. *Harmony Ideology: Justice and Control in a Zapotec Mountain Village*. Stanford, CA: Stanford University Press.

Noble, Cinnie. 2012. *Conflict Management Coaching: The CINERGY™ Model*. Toronto: CINERGY™ Coaching.

Picard, Cheryl Ann. 2000. "The Many Meanings of Mediation: A Sociological Study of Mediation in Canada." PhD diss., Carleton University.

Picard, Cheryl. 2002. *Mediating Interpersonal and Small Group Conflict*, updated and rev. ed. Ottawa: Golden Dog Press.

Picard, Cheryl. 2003a. "Learning about Learning: The Value of Insight." *Conflict Resolution Quarterly* 20 (4): 477–84.

Picard, Cheryl. 2003b. "Why Mediators Mediate." *Alternative Dispute Resolution Practice Manual* 1 (June): 1501–84.

Picard, Cheryl, and Marnie Jull. 2011. "Learning through Deepening Conversations: A Key Insight Mediation Strategy." *Conflict Resolution Quarterly* 29 (2): 151–76.

Picard, Cheryl, and Kenneth Melchin. 2007. "Insight Mediation: A Learning Centered Mediation Model." *Negotiation Journal* 23 (1): 35–54.

Picard, Cheryl, and Janet Siltanen. 2013. "Exploring the Significance of Emotion for Mediation Practice." *Conflict Resolution Quarterly* 31 (1): 31–55.

Price, Jamie. 2013. "Explaining Human Conflict: Human Needs Theory and the Insight Approach." In *Conflict Resolution and Human Needs: Linking Theory to Practice*, ed. Kevin Avruch and Christopher Mitchell, 108–23. New York: Routledge.

Rawls, John. 1971. *A Theory of Justice*. Cambridge, MA: Harvard University Press.

Ross, Lee, David Greene, and Pamela House. 1977. "The 'False Consensus Effect': An Egocentric Bias in Social Perception and Attribution Processes." *Journal of Experimental Social Psychology* 13 (3): 279–301.

Sandel, Michael. 1982. *Liberalism and the Limits of Justice*. Cambridge: Cambridge University Press.

Sargent, Neil, Cheryl Picard, and Marnie Jull. 2011. "Rethinking Conflict: Perspectives from the Insight Approach." *Negotiation Journal* 27 (3): 343–66.

Schon, Donald A. 1083. *The Reflective Practitioner: How Professionals Think in Action*. New York: Basic Books.

Shriver, Sargent. 1966. Address to the Illinois State Bar Association, Chicago, 16 June. Available online at http://www.sargentshriver.org/speech-article/address-to-the-illinois-state-bar-association.

Smith, M.K. 1999, 2011. "What Is Praxis?' *Encyclopaedia of Informal Education*. Available online at http://www.infed.org/biblio/b-praxis.htm.

Taylor, Charles. 1989. *Sources of the Self: The Making of the Modern Identity*. Cambridge, MA: Harvard University Press.

Taylor, Charles. 1992. *The Ethics of Authenticity*. Cambridge, MA: Harvard University Press.

Tidwell, Allan. 1997. "Problem Solving for One." *Mediation Quarterly* 14 (4): 309–17.

Tolman, Edward C. 1948. "Cognitive Maps in Rats and Men." *Psychological Review* 55 (4): 189–208.

United States. 2011. Federal Bureau of Investigation. "Uniform Report: Expanded Homicide Data." Washington, DC. Available online at http://www.fbi.gov/about-us/cjis/ucr/crime-in-the-u.s/2011/crime-in-the-u.s.-2011/tables/.

United States. 2015. Centers for Disease Control and Prevention. "WISQUARS: Nonfatal Injury Reports, 2001–2013." Atlanta, GA. Available online at http://webappa.cdc.gov/sasweb/ncipc/nfirates2001.html.

Vogt, Eric E., Juanita Brown, and David Isaacs. 2003. *The Art of Powerful Questions: Catalyzing Insight, Innovation, and Action*. Mill Valley, CA: Whole Systems Associates.

Winslade, John, and Gerald Monk. 2000. *Narrative Mediation*. San Francisco: Jossey-Bass.

Zuckerman, Miron. 1979. "Attribution of Success and Failure Revisited, or: The Motivational Bias Is Alive and Well in Attribution Theory." *Journal of Personality* 47 (2): 245–87.

Index